UNITED KINGDOM COMPARATIVE LAW SERIES

VOLUME 6

KV-621-758

# Comparative Product Liability

edited by

## *C. J. Miller*

*Professor of Law,*
*University of Warwick*

*Based on revised papers and contributions originally*
*submitted to a colloquium held by the United Kingdom*
*National Committee for Comparative Law at the*
*University of Edinburgh*

1986

K953

© 1986 The British Institute of International and Comparative Law

ISBN 0 903067-28-5

QUEEN MARY
COLLEGE
LIBRARY

Printed in Great Britain by The Chameleon Press Limited
5-25 Burr Road, Wandsworth, London SW18 4SG.

QMC 725133 6

a30213 007251336b

# Comparative
# Product Liability

DATE DUE FOR RETURN

New accession
6/1/88

30 JUN 1990

30. NOV 92

APR 93

MAY 93

27.     93

16. JUN 93

30-Sep-93
(AP)

APR 94

19 JAN 1996

WITHDRAWN
FROM STOCK
QMUL LIBRARY

*The United Kingdom Comparative Law Series is produced by the United Kingdom National Committee of Comparative Law and published by the British Institute of International and Comparative Law.*

TABLE OF CONTENTS

## NOTES ON CONTRIBUTORS

### C.J. MILLER

C.J. Miller is Professor of Law in the University of Warwick. He is the joint author of *Product Liability* (1977) and *Consumer Law: Cases and Materials* (1985) and the author of *Product Liability and Safety Encyclopaedia* (1979-86).

### HANS CLAUDIUS TASCHNER

Dr. Hans Claudius Taschner holds degrees from the Universities of Mainz, Paris, Freiburg and New York. He is an honorary Professor in the University of Saarbrücken. He has been an official of the European Commission since 1964 and, since 1974, head of the division on approximation of legislation, product liability. Since 1979 he has been head of the division on civil and economic law, criminal law and law of procedure and citizens' rights.

### FERDINANDO ALBANESE

Dr. Ferdinando Albanese is Deputy Director of Legal Affairs in the Council of Europe. He holds the following degrees and qualifications: Dottore in Giurisprudenza (Messina), Diploma in International Relations (SAIS of the John Hopkins University, Bologna Center), Master of Laws (Yale Law School), Institut de Droit Comparé (Paris). Dr. Albanese has written several articles in the field of product liability, reservation of title, bankruptcy and medical law.

### AUBREY L. DIAMOND

Aubrey Diamond is Professor Emeritus of Law in the University of London, and was formerly Director of the Institute of Advanced Legal Studies. He was a Member of the Law Commission from 1971-76 and Chairman of the Anglo-Scottish Working Party on Product Liability. He is the joint author of *The Consumer, Society and the Law* (4th ed. 1981), and the author of *Commercial and Consumer Credit: An Introduction* (1982).

### PETER CANE

Peter Cane is tutor in law at Corpus Christi College, Oxford. He has written several articles about recovery for economic loss in tort, and is co-author of an Australian textbook of tort law.

*GENEVIEVE VINEY*

Geneviève Viney is Professor of Law in the University of Paris 1 (Panthéon-Sorbonne). She has written extensively on the law of contract, tort and product liability. Her principal publications include *Le Déclin de la Responsibilité Individuelle* (1965) and *La Responsabilité*, Vol 1 - Conditions (1982). She is joint author of *La Réparation du Dommage Corporel* (1985).

*SPIRO SIMITIS*

Dr. Spiro Simitis is Professor of Law (civil and labour law) in the University of Frankfurt. He was rapporteur of the German Lawyers' Association and a member of its board on product liability. He is a member of the Private International Law Committee and a consultant to the Federal government. He is also Data Protection Commissioner of the State of Hesse. He has written extensively on the law of contract, tort and on data protection law.

*JAN HELLNER*

Jan Hellner is Professor Emeritus of Law in the University of Stockholm. He has participated in the preparation of legislation in consumer protection and insurance law and has written extensively on insurance and tort law. His most recent publications including *Specielle avtalsrätt I. Köprätt* (1982), *Speciell avtalsrätt II. Kontraktsrätt* (1984) and *Skadesatämdsrätt* (1985). He has also contributed to *Medical Responsibility in Western Europe* (eds. Deutsch and Schreiber), 1985.

*JERRY J. PHILLIPS*

Jerry J. Phillips is the W.P. Toms Professor of Law at the University of Tennessee College of Law in Knoxville, Tennessee, USA. He holds the degrees of AB and JD (Yale University) and MA (Cambridge University). He is a member of Phi Beta Kappa, an advisor to Phi Delta Phi, and a member of the American Law Institute. He has been an adviser to the Tennessee Law Revision Commission and to the United States Task Force on Products Liability. He is the author of an American Casebook on the law of torts, two books on the law of products liability, and a two-volume treatise on products liability. In addition, he has written numerous articles on torts and products liability law.

*S.M. WADDAMS*

S.M. Waddams is Professor of Law in the University of Toronto, research director of the Ontario Law Reform Commission project on products liability, and the author of books on products liability, contracts and damages.

# INTRODUCTION

*C.J. Miller*

The annual colloquium of the United Kingdom National Committee of Comparative Law was held in New Senate Hall, Old College, in the University of Edinburgh on 18 and 19 September, 1984. The topic was Product Liability. This book consists of revised versions of the papers which were presented at the colloquium which I had the pleasure of organising and chairing, In this I benefited from the admirable assistance of the Committee's secretary, Mr. Keith Hendry of the University of Birmingham, and of Professor Neil McCormick and his colleagues from the University of Edinburgh. The colloquium was attended by some sixty or more participants, including representatives from the academic world, consumer groups, the European Economic Communities, the Council of Europe, the Office of Fair Trading and the Department of Trade and Industry.

During the period leading up to the conference, and indeed during the conference itself, there was a widespread feeling that the long awaited reforms of product liability laws within Europe had effectively ground to a halt. The Council of Europe or Strasbourg Convention on Products Liability in Regard to Personal Injury and Death had been adopted in September 1976, but it attracted few signatories since the focus of attention had by then shifted to proposals which were under discussion in the Commission of the EEC. Here, it must be said, progress was painfully slow. Indeed, there were many who believed that the differing views of Member States were so irreconcilable that the Council of Ministers would not reach agreement within the foreseeable future. In retrospect the extended delays were not surprising. Product liability has its roots in contract (or sales) law and the law of tort or delict where there are marked differences between the approaches of civil and common law systems. Obviously, such differences constituted an obstacle to the approximation of the laws of Member States. Moreover the subject is one in which there was bound to be strong and effective opposition from industry to any attempt to facilitate recovery through the imposition of a system of strict liability. Such a system had been adopted in the United States of America and the opinion of industry was that the results gave considerable cause for concern, not least because of the escalation in insurance premiums which had followed.

The general pessimism among would-be reformers finally lifted in the spring and summer of 1985 when there was relatively rapid and unexpected progress towards agreement on the terms of the Council Directive of 25 July 1985 (No. 87/374/EEC) on the approximation of the laws, regulations and administrative provisions of the Member States concerning liability for defective products.(Appendix A, p. 173)

Admittedly, the agreement was not without the costs which accompany any compromise. Indeed some may take the view that the Directive was deprived of much of its utility by the expedient of adopting optional provisions for the major areas of controversy: namely, the position of primary agricultural products, the defence for defects which were not discoverable in the then state of scientific and technical knowledge, and the question of a ceiling on damage for design defects. This is not a view which I share, although clearly such optional provisions must detract from the justification for the Directive, that is the harmonisation of laws within the Community. Be that as it may, the Directive must be implemented within three years of its notification to Member States and hence by 30 July 1988. In the case of the United Kingdom this will involve primary legislation, rather than delegated legislation made under the European Communities Act 1972. It is likely that such legislation will be introduced in the 1986-87 Parliamentary session.

The provisions of the Directive have changed quite significantly through its various drafts so that they now have much more in common with those of the Convention (Appendix B, p.185).This comparison is the main subject of Dr. Albanese's paper. The justifications for the principle of strict liability on which the Directive is based are explored in the first part of Dr. Taschner's paper which also contains a helpful analysis of the scope of the so called "state of the art" qualification to strict liability. As Dr. Taschner explains, this qualification may embody two related ideas. One is the accepted principle that the standard of defectiveness should be based on that prevailing when the product was put into circulation and not on that which had been achieved when the damage occurred or the action was heard. Article 6 of the Directive is to

this effect. The other principle is more controversial and addresses the relevance of an alleged
inability to discover the existence of a danger.
Article 7 contains an optional provision, which the
United Kingdom government is committed to introducing, whereby "The producer shall not be liable as a
result of this Directive if he proves .... (e) that
the state of scientific and technical knowledge at
the time when he put the product into circulation
was not such as to enable the existence of the
defect to be discovered". This wording suggests a
very limited defence based on the overall state of
scientific and technical knowledge at the relevant
time. Presumably the defence should fail if it
appears that the defect had in fact been discovered,
albeit in an experiment in some distant land which
was written up only in an obscure journal. However,
interested parties, including representatives of consumer organisations, will pay particular attention
to the precise form of words used in the implementing Act. A tightly drafted defence could all too
easily become one which might be satisfied on
proving that all reasonable precautions had been
exercised.

As is explained in Professor Diamond's paper,
the principle of strict liability is not a novel concept in this area of English law. Indeed it has
been a feature of the Sale of Goods Act for many
years, extending even to the scientifically undiscoverable risk. This will continue after the implementation of the Directive which specifically states
in Article 13 that it "shall not affect any rights
which an injured person may have according to the
rules of the law of contractual or non-contractual
liability". Of course the problem is that such
rights benefit only the party to the contract and
not others who may be injured by the goods, including members of the family and bystanders. Professor
Diamond's paper also addresses the difficult issue
of whether all producers should be included within
the scope of the Directive's regime, or whether an
exception should be made for producers of natural
products, components or pharmaceutical products. In
the case of primary agricultural products, it is now
known that the United Kingdom government will avail
itself of the option of excluding them from the
scope of the implementing Act.

The principal concern of the Directive is with
damage in the form of death or personal injury and
there is general agreement that this is the area in
which the law is most in need of harmonisation and
reform. The Directive applies also to damage to

property of a type ordinarily intended for private use or consumption although not to damage to the defective product itself. It has no application to other types of property damage or economic loss where recovery will continue to be governed by the general law of tort and contract. As Peter Cane's paper makes clear this area is one of considerable uncertainty, where the courts are still struggling to find coherent principles to stake out the boundaries of contract and tort. Many of the recent important cases have involved defects in real property, rather than in products, presumably because the sums involved, especially in latent damage claims, are usually that much greater. Nonetheless there are clear parallels between the two situations. The general trend of the latest cases is to curtail the extension of liability which might have developed from the decision of the House of Lords in *Junior Books Ltd. v Veitchi Co. Ltd.*

The two essays which follow are contributed by Professors Viney and Simitis, writing from the perspective of French and German law respectively. As Professor Viney's essay makes clear, French law is already quite familiar with the imposition of strict liability on the producers or manufacturers of defective products. The "hidden defect" principle and the *action directe* are capable of achieving this result. Her essay also illustrates the valuable work of such bodies as the Consumer Law Revision Committee. The essay contributed by Professor Simitis similarly explores the contractual and delictual routes to strict liability in the context of the German Civil Code. It also contains a detailed examination of the underlying rationale of strict liability and of some of the policy problems associated with it.

Professor Hellner's essay notes that Swedish law is still "groping hesitantly with a number of problems" and that its major contribution lies in its pharmaceutical injuries insurance scheme. Industrial accidents also are covered by insurance through a social security scheme. Although such schemes have their limitations and associated problems, there is no doubt that many find them preferable as an alternative to the hazards and delays of litigation. One result is of course that attention may then shift to the difficult areas of property damage and economic loss and to the borderline between the two. It seems that this has happened in Sweden.

The final two essays are from the North American continent and they are contributed by Professors Jerry Phillips and Steven Waddams respectively. As is well known, the courts of the United States of America have long been at the forefront of the debate in staking out the bounds of strict liability in the common law world. In the relatively early years of this development their judgments illustrated that, contrary to the assumptions of many, strict liability did not lead to automatic recovery on the part of injured consumers. The requirements of causation and of establishing that the product was "defective" often proved troublesome. These problems are still with us, but they have been joined by such difficult areas as mass tort litigation and successor corporate liability. The point is of course that corporate bankruptcy or voluntary liquidation may, as in the asbestos litigation, not infrequently follow upon multiple claims. Similar issues are addressed by Professor Simitis when he notes that it is not sufficient for regulations simply to establish liability. There must also be a realistic chance of compensation.

The Canadian experience in the common law provinces is also of particular interest as is seen in Professor Waddam's essay. Here the common law background of *Donoghue v Stevenson* has been supplemented by legislation, much of which builds on the early work of the Ontario Law Reform Commission in its Report on Consumer Warranties and Guarantees in the Sale of Goods (1972). However the approach seems less than satisfactory as it is often linked to a breach of a statutory warranty or to damage resulting from a "consumer product". As Professor Waddam's essay illustrates, such an approach can all too often lead to unacceptable anomalies. The approach of the EEC Directive seems preferable, although admittedly it is limited in the types of damage which it covers.

By way of conclusion to these introductory remarks, it is hoped that readers will find that this volume of essays offers a timely and valuable contribution to what will inevitably be a continuing debate. In the European context, product liability has come of age with the making of the Directive. It seems entirely safe to predict that it will remain in the forefront of legal debate for many years to come.

Finally, I should like to than those who contributed to the success of the conference for which these essays were originally written. I am indebted also to Philip Britton for his admirable translation of Professor Viney's essay and to Anne Goldstein for her invaluable assistance in the production of the book.

## EUROPEAN INITIATIVES: THE EUROPEAN COMMUNITIES

*Dr Hans Claudius Taschner\**

*In memory of John D B Mitchell.*

*Professor Mitchell was the Director of the Centre of European Governmental Studies of this University of Edinburgh, a centre for research on and teaching of European Community law. Hundreds of Edinburgh students and young administrators have studied this new developing area of law there. For many years he organised monthly conferences on current topics relevant to the law of his country, to the law of the European Communities and to the relationship between the two. "The legal consequences of Great Britain's entry in the Common Market" and the "Two-tier-Board system and workers' participation" were the issues on which the author had the honour to make a contribution.*

*John Mitchell was a convinced European. He was a fighter for the idea of European integration even if it was sometimes not very convenient to fly the European flag. In remembering him, all who believe in European integration owe him a strong debt of gratitude for all he has done because of his European Convictions.*

---

\*    The author wishes to make it clear that the opinions expressed in this contribution are his own and in no way binding on the Commission of the European Communities.

## 1.    Introduction

The "United Kingdom Committee on Comparative Law" is
the sister organisation of the French "Société des
législations comparées" and the German "Gesellschaft
für Rechtsvergleichung", sharing with those
associations a high reputation. This year it has
organised an academic conference on product
liability. This is unlike the many others on the
same topic where the lobbying interest of the
organiser, the selection of the speakers, and the
choice of special questions to be discussed
determine the results of the conference in advance.
This conference is orientated only towards
comparative law, and its participants' interests are
solely academic. Therefore it is not necessary to
repeat for the umpteenth time the basic
considerations which have led to the European
Community's initiative and the defence of the draft
directive. These have been set out and published,
most recently in Chapter VIII of Geoffrey
Woodroffe's *Consumer Law in the EEC* in which the
reader may find the publication of the contributions
made to the Conference of the Society of Public
Teachers of Law last September in Bristol. The ups
and downs of the political discussions which have
taken place over the past few years in the EC
institutions responsible for the task prescribed by
the EEC Treaty as "approximation of legislation" are
of little interest. Positions change too often.
The necessity to reach a unanimous decision on the
Commission's proposal opens the door, as usual, to
endless negotiations. The political impact and the
natural tendency to work out compromises are surely
not factors likely to preserve the well balanced and
inter dependent system of rules originally proposed
by the Commission with the assistance of four
countries' most learned experts in the matter.

## 2.    The Principles of the Directive (Appendix A,p.173)

On 25 July 1985 the Council of the European Communities adopted the Directive on the approximation of
the laws, regulations and administrative provisions
of the Member States concerning liability for
defective products. The Directive is based on the
following principles: The producer is strictly
liable. There is, in principle, no ceiling on
liability. As regards the damage resulting from
death or personal injury, caused by identical items
with the same defect, any Member State may,
however, restrict such liability over a ten-year
period to an overall amount of not less than 70
million European Currency Units (ECU), that is about

£40 million. There is no provision for a financial
limit to liability in individual cases: it is
therefore precluded. Neither is a ceiling for
damage to property possible under the Directive. On
expiry of the ten-year period, that is 30 July 1995,
the Council will decide - in the light of a report
and proposal submitted by the Commission - whether
that option should cease and unlimited strict
liability be introduced also in those Member States
which have made use of it. Strict liability is
limited in time. It lapses ten years after the
producer put the product which caused the damage
into circulation. The producer is liable for damage
caused by death, for personal injuries and damage to
property; in the latter case, however, only where the
item damaged was utilised in a private capacity.
Damage to property in the commercial sphere is
excluded. The Directive lays down a lower
threshold of 500 ECU, that is about £280 for
damages to private property so as to exclude
trivial damage.

The producer is, in principle, not liable if
the defect existed at the time the product was put
into circulation, but could not be discovered as the
general state of scientific and technical knowledge
at that time was not adequate to make such
discovery possible and this can be proven (no liability for "development risks"). Member States are
free to derogate from this principle by retaining
(in the case of the German Drugs Act) or introducing appropriate legislation. In the latter case,
the Commission is entitled to attempt to embody the
proposed measure in Community legislation and
submit it to the Council as a proposal to amend the
Directive. At all events, in ten years' time the
Council will decide, as in the case of the review
of the limit on total liability for personal injury
and following the submission of a report and
proposal by the Commission, whether in the interests
of greater legal uniformity such exclusion of
liability can be abolished in all Member States.

3.    Approximation of Laws

One of the tasks of European institutions, of the
European Communities as well as of the Council of
Europe, is "to approximate Member States' laws", as
laid down in Art 100 of the EEC Treaty, or "to
achieve greater unity between its Member States", as
in the preamble to the Council of Europe's Convention on Product Liability. (Appendix B, p. 185)

"Approximation of legislation" or "unification

of laws" presupposes, in general, existing statutory regulations or case rules in a determined area which are the object of those activities. But this is not necessarily so. It may well be that the rules elaborated and agreed by the responsible European institutions, which will guide or "direct" the intended legal evolution in the states concerned, are unknown, new, and progressive with respect to existing national laws. To approximate laws does not simply mean to find a solution midway between the severest and the laxest of all existing national rules. The task consists of preparing and adopting the most appropriate rule with respect to the interests involved and the needs of society, in order to regulate a certain domain of law such as product liability. For this reason, approximation or unification of laws is also necessarily law reform.

This activity which the European institutions have not chosen themselves but with which they have been charged by the agreement of the states involved, is difficult due to another aspect: it introduces law reform not only for one state, but for all states which are members of the relevant institution. The inherent necessity to have regard not only to one or two other "foreign" states with possibly different social and economic structures, but to many such states increases the natural unwillingness to proceed with law reform. This unwillingness is itself always a very serious obstacle. The conclusion to be drawn from this finding is clearly that the steps to be made towards new rules should not be too great, otherwise inertia will prevent any steps being made at all.

Given these premises, and in order to discuss more academically theoretical basic principles of product liability in the context of law reform not only in this country, but in all western European states belonging to the Council of Europe and the European Communities, this contribution to the Conference concentrates on two major problems of product liability, namely the kind of liability to be envisaged and the notions of "development risks" and the "state of the art" defence.

In doing so, the "functional approach" to comparative law developed by Ernst Rabel will be followed, leaving aside the fairly sterile "institutional method". The latter method compares legal institutions, systems built by statute law or even simple terms themselves, whilst the former - with which lawyers in common law countries will feel more

at ease - formulates a concrete case as a phenomenon
of daily life and asks how the national laws to be
compared would deal with it.

## 4.    A Case for Discussion

Turning to the first issue, the kind of liability,
the following case is suggested for discussion: a
producer of tyres puts a new range on the market
advertising them as being specially made for fast
cars: "Monza Steel tyres - for your car, for you the
fast driver, for your safety as a fast driver!" He
admits that in the ordinary process of tyre production it is technically impossible to produce a 100%
safe production, 0.05% of all tyres coming off the
line having unavoidable and undiscoverable amalgama-
tion failures in the material used. These
deficiencies cause disruptions between the tread of
the tyres and the tyre body, leading to explosions,
usually when the tyres are used at high speed.
Should the producer be liable for the foreseeable,
but virtually unavoidable accidents which result?

Liability for fault presupposes the possibility
that a free man could avoid causing damage by acting
in a way which, in the normal course of events,
would not lead to any damage. "A duty to take care"
is required in planning activities. The extent of
this duty is determined according to the standards
one finds in society, for example, the ideal "pater
familias" of the Roman law or, transferred to modern
time, "le bon père de famille". The violation of
these standards, which is qualified as "negligence",
serves as a reason for liability. Consequently,
liability is denied if the necessary duty to take
care has been respected, because what the accused
person has done would have been done by the "pater
familias" as well.

This fundamental distinction was the great
achievement of the legal evolution which began in
the 17th century as a result of the theory called
"natural law" ("Naturrecht") and culminated in the
19th century. In France, the famous legal writer
Dumat stood for this. The great European codifications which took place around the end of the 18th or
the beginning of the 19th century, the "Allgemeines
Landrecht", the general law of the state in Prussia,
the French "code civil" or the Austrian civil code,
are all based on the fault principle. Later on in
the 19th century, it was one of the bases for
economic and industrial progress as it set new
activities free from undue liability. Damage falling
outside the limits of taking the required care were

accidents  to be  suffered  by  the   unfortunate victims
as Acts of God.

In the case described one could find  sufficient
elements  to  establish a violation of  the  required
duty  to  take care and therefore the  negligence  of
the  producer: how could he advertise a new  type  of
tyre as being specially safe for fast car drivers  if
he  knows  that under typical  production  conditions
0.05%  of  tyres  will  be  unavoidable  unsafe?  The
standards used to determine the duty which has to  be
respected are obviously vague. They can be made  more
severe, they can be stretched, they can even be overstretched  beyond  reasonable  understanding.  For
example,  to have placed a car's fuel tank where  it
created  an unreasonably high risk – perhaps  against
better  advice, giving rise to greater expense  –  as
in the  Ford-Pinto  case in the United States,  could
easily  have been taken as the basis of a  claim  for
negligence.  The  same  is  true  in  the  German
thalidomide  case.  When a company discovers a  new
pharmaceutical substance with excellent qualities  as
a  tranquilliser  for nervous  persons,  should  this
company  not,  indeed  must  it  not,  take  into
consideration  a  certain  category  of  potentially
nervous  persons,  pregnant  women,  and  test  the
effects  of  this new substance on the  human  embryo
before  it  puts the drug on the  market?  Are  such
effects absolutely unforeseeable? The answer is  no.
One  cannot  therefore consider this case to be  the
model case of development risk liability as has been,
with  all  respect,  wrongly  considered  by  the  two
British Law Commissions.

This leads to the conclusion that liability  for
fault  would solve many cases of  product  liability,
and the trends in some jurisdictions during the  last
few decades to reverse the onus probandi are only  an
extension  of  the standards as to the duty  to  take
care, masked by a procedural legal instrument.

For  these reasons, is has  been  impossible  to
understand  the outcry from most producers when  the
Council  of  Europe and the Commission  tabled  their
proposals.  The "revolution" in this area for  which
both international organisations were blamed did  not
start  in 1976 or 1977 with the publication of  these
texts,  but  years earlier and silently  when  courts
changed  their  understanding  of the  duty  to  take
care,  as  in  Germany  in  November  1968 when  the
"chicken-pest" case was decided.

But one can approach our case for discussion  by
emphasising the other, more objective, aspect of  its

circumstances, namely the fact that a certain, very small proportion of all tyres produced will be unavoidably defective, due to the production conditions which, with the best of intentions, cannot be improved. This element of chance obliges one to consider the risk inherent in the case. If it is said that this result cannot, with the best of intentions, be avoided, one cannot cover this case by applying liability for fault. The normal reaction to a risk would be to abstain from all acts which create the risk. But this necessarily means giving up at the same time the positive aspects of those activities. One is, therefore, faced with the question of to whom this risk should be allocated; to the person who has caused it or to the person who has suffered from it?

If the principle of liability for fault even in the circumstances described is defended, one necessarily comes to the conclusion that the risk must be borne by the victim alone. But the justification put forward in the 19th century, namely to keep young industrial enterprises free from excessively heavy liability charges, has lost its significance. Indeed, there are many reasons to decide the other way round and the best of them seems to be that this allocation of risk to the victim is simply unjust. If the advantages of modern sophisticated, but necessary, products are available for everybody, why should the relatively small inconveniences be borne by the unfortunate individuals who are struck by the chance circumstance of being the user of the one product which is, among thousands, defective? The answer is clear: the risk should be borne by the producer who has the possibility of spreading the cost of the damages paid over all users of non-defective products. The instrument for allocating the risk in this way is to submit the producer to a system of strict liability. The answer that society has given to the problem of abstaining from all acts bearing a risk and the consequent giving up of the profitable aspects of those acts is correct. The person wishing to carry out a risky activity is allowed to do so, for his personal benefit and for the benefit of society, but he is required to accept responsibility for all detrimental consequences of the risks so created. The Roman praetor allowed the farmer to use his horse to carry fruit and vegetables at the Forum Romanum. This method of transport increased the range of goods on offer to society and, for the farmer, increased the possibility for personal profit, but nevertheless created the risk of damage whenever the horse followed its unpredictable nature. The praetor did not, however, accept the farmer's excuse that as the horse had never before gone out of control, the damage caused was unforeseeable. To allow the activity, but to allocate the risk, this "yes, but ..." approach is socially the best solution, even if the aspect that society at large profits at the same time (and perhaps to the same degree) as the producer, from the activity leads some legal writers to plead for compensation of the victim to be met by society. The modern economic system, based on individual initiative, profit-making, and social responsibility should not follow such ideas, but be proud to accept the equitable solution of the Roman praetor.

These considerations have led in Continental codifications to the strict liability of the owner of an animal or a chattel which gives rise to the risk of damage - Art 1384 s 1 Code civil, Art 1905 Codigo civil, Art 2052 Codice civile and, to a limited extent, s 833 German Civil code. These same considerations have also led to strict liability provisions for a company using nuclear energy leading to damage. Furthermore, in some countries like Germany, the same means have been used to solve the problems of road accidents, air traffic accidents, railroad accidents or accidents caused by the transportation of energy over land.

Because the criteria for strict liability - unavoidably risky activity of public interest - are given, the same considerations should be applied to solve the earlier case: the producer of tyres with a defect rate of 0.05% should be allowed to continue his production - provided he does not try to evade liability for damage by claiming that it did not result from a "breach of duty", i.e. "negligence".

This solution obviously applies to construction defects. However, it also applies to design defects in so far as the reproach of production without due care cannot be made. The risk associated with untried products, mainly new products, cannot be transferred to the user, but the part to be played by fault liability in this area is and should be much greater than in the area of construction defects.

This solution does not apply in the last area involving "instruction defects" or "lack of warnings". Here, no unavoidable risk is involved. How far a producer has to warn the potential users of a product is a question of their possible experience in its use. The newer a product, the greater the need to warn, and the greater the duty to do so. The breach of this duty is a breach of the duty to take care and, therefore, ordinary negligence. As always, it would be better to go a little bit further than is normally required. However the standards to be followed have to be determined by the courts. This is a matter of ordinary fault liability. It is not, for example, suggested that the users of electric hairdryers must be warned not to use them when taking a bath (water and electricity forming a fatal combination as everybody knows); nor is it required to put a skull and crossbones on the French perfume "Chanel No. 5", simply because perfume is an inflammable product, as once again, everybody knows.

To sum up: product liability cases can, to a large extent, be solved by applying fault liability principles. Both European proposals maintain this liability (Art 13 Directive, Art 12 Council of Europe Convention). The duty of care used to establish negligence should, nevertheless, not be overstretched. The heart of product liability remains the problem of causing damage by creating unavoidable risks. This is the case with construction defects and, to a lesser extent, design defects. Such risks should be allocated to the producer by introducing a system of strict liability. Both European proposals base their system of guiding the approximation of laws and law reform on strict liability (Art 1 Directive, Art 3 s 1 Council of Europe Convention). The cases of instruction defects or "lack of warnings" can be satisfactorily solved by applying fault liability.

5.    Development Risks and the State of the Art

The terms "development risk" and "state-of-the-art" defence seem to be unclear, even, as experience shows, in common-law countries where they were developed. They are unknown in codified law countries. Literal translations such as "risque de développement" or "Entwicklungsrisiken" are too broad and imprecise to have any meaning. The new German Pharmaceutical Act of 1976, the first statutory law on product liability in Europe, does not use the term. The same is true of the new Israeli law on defective products liability of 17 March 1980. It is not believed that much help can be had by finding out what the term may mean in certain jurisdictions; what has to be done is to discuss cases in order to agree solutions.

The two following cases are suggested for consideration:

The producer of certain products, e.g. pharmaceutical products, puts a new drug on the market. He has carried out all the tests known at the time of production as to possible harmful effects. The tests show the probability of some acceptable side-effects, but no risk of detrimental harm. Years after the first sale, it appears that this drug causes a certain type of cancer. New scientific methods developed in ; the meantime show a clear causal connection between the drug and the disease. Should the producer be liable for the damage caused?

The producer of another product, e.g. a car, puts a vehicle on the market in 1978 without special safety devices, such as head-restraints or safety belts, known, but not customary, at that time. In 1981, the same producer adds those devices in series of cars of a new production run. One year later, a driver of a 1978 model has an accident, the damage in which was mainly caused by the absence of the aforementioned safety devices. Should the producer be liable for this damage?

The analysis of those two cases leads us to the following two findings:

In the first case it may be found that the product was defective at the moment it was put into circulation, in the second it was not. The decisive moment to determine whether the product in issue was defective or not is the day on which it was put into circulation. Product liability is liability of the producer for a defective product which was defective from the very beginning. There is no liability if the product was not defective at the time of being put on the market, but later became defective.

When one asks in the first case whether the product was defective because it has the ability to cause cancer, to-day and at the day it was marketed for the first time, the answer is yes. The fact that it caused cancer at the time of the first sale was a non-fulfilment of the safety standards the public was - at the time of first marketing - "entitled to expect", as it is formulated in the definitions of defect in the Convention (Art 2 c) and in the Directive (Art 6). The judge has to put himself in this situation. He is not asked to determine defectiveness at the moment the damage was caused.

In the second case, the car without safety devices was not defective at the moment of pro- duction, because it was not the normal safety standard of cars produced in 1978 to have head- restraints or safety belts. Because it was not a normal safety standard, the higher degree of safety provided for since 1981 could not legitimately be expected by the user. If there was a risk of damage in 1978, that risk was known. It was accepted, because we know that a car is - even to-day - an inherently risky means of transport. The car was not defective. Therefore the producer is not liable.

The non-defective car did not become defective when the producer, years later, fitted new models with those safety devices. If such an interpreta- tion was the consequence of improving products to provide higher quality, no producer would do so, because he would consequently be obliged to recall from the market all existing products not meeting the new standard. The product did not change between 1978 and 1981. What had changed were the safety expectations and, side by side, the technical standards related to those safety expectations. In 1981, these expectations became legitimate, so that cars without these safety standards were defective.

The second finding relates only to the first case. This case constitutes only a variation of the normal product liability cases in the category of design defects. In ordinary product liability cases the defect in the product might not be discovered by its producer applying ordinary methods of testing, but it cannot be excluded that more satisfactory test results could be obtained by using better technical or scientific methods. The special criteria of the drug case is that, due to the absolute lack of scientific and technological knowledge, the existing defect could not be discovered by anyone. But the defect, the carcinogenic property, existed at the time of pro- duction, and was a defect because the consumer of a pharmaceutical product was, also at that time, entitled to expect the security of not receiving a carcinogenic product.

If one would like to put labels on both solu- tions by using terms, it could be suggested, with all necessary care, that one speaks of:

- "development risk liability" in the situation described in the first case, and

- "state of the art" defence in the second.

That "state of the art" is not a "defence" in the strict sense, but the qualification of the product as being defective or not, made by the judge in deciding the case, has been taken into consideration.

As far as the "European initiatives" with respect to these two cases are concerned, for which solutions have to be found, the positions are as follows:

For the drug case, which could now be described as a case involving a "development risk", the Commission originally proposed holding the producer liable. This was laid down in Art 1, s 2 of the 1976 proposal which reads:

"The producer shall be liable even if the article could not have been regarded as defective in the light of scientific and technological development at the time when he put the article into circulation."

The Council decided, in principle not to include the "development risk" in the liability of the producer. But it formulated this exclusion as a defence, putting the *onus probandi* on his shoulders. Indeed, art 7(e) provides that:

the producer shall not be liable as a result of this Directive if he proves

. . . . . . . .

(e)      that the state of scientific and technical knowledge at the time when he put the product into circulation was not such as to enable the existence of the defect to be discovered; ...."

As has been said, Member States are free to derogate from this principle by introducing appropriate legislation, provided that they follow the procedure laid down in Art 15, s 2.

The position of the Council of Europe Convention is the same as originally proposed by the Commission. Art 3, s 1 states the principle of strict liability. Art 5 enumerates its exceptions or "defences" - "defence" because the *onus probandi* as

to these exceptions lies with the producer - and
there is no defence of "development risk" mentioned
in this article. This interpretation is confirmed
by the Explanatory Report which states in its
section 41 that the expert committee decided "that
development risk should not be an exception to
producer's liability".

With respect to the "state of the art", defence
as described, the Commission proposed not to hold
the producer liable in circumstances such as those
discussed in the second case. To make it clear
that there should be no liability - because the
product was not defective - the definition of defect
as proposed in Art 4 of the original draft was
enlarged in 1979 by adding the words "taking into
account ... the time at which it (i.e. the product)
was put into circulation". This formulation makes
it clear that the decisive moment in determining
whether the product causing the damage was defective
is the moment of putting it into circulation. This
solution, excluding any liability in this case by
denying its defective character, is justified
because no producer can be expected to be liable for
a product which met with the safety requirements at
the moment of production and was therefore not
defective even although the safety requirements
changed later. Liability in such a case would
hinder innovation and would lead to costly and
uninsurable recall obligations. This has now been
adopted by the Council in Art 6 of the Directive.

The same solution would apply under the Council
of Europe Convention because Art 2 (c), which
defines the defect, also refers to "having regard to
all the circumstances". These "circumstances"
include the time of putting the article into
circulation.

The result is that the "state of the art" defence is, understood as described, provided for in
both European legal instruments. The legislator or
the legislators are free to decide how far liability
should go in the first case, the drug case. They can
include or exclude the "development risk" but they
cannot change the basic principles of the respective
legal systems.

6.  Act of God

The contribution to this conference can be concluded
by suggesting that an exclusion of liability for
"development risk", as described, cannot be
justified by pretending that the cause of the damage

can be described as an "Act of God","force majeure" or "höhere Gewalt" and by applying this principle. The author would not dare to discuss this question in common law. The following remarks concentrate on French and German law only.

Under French law, "force majeure" has been developed as a cause of exoneration in the domain of contractual obligations. The relevant provisions are Arts 1147 and 1148 of the Code civil. The principle has been extended to the law of torts. It is true that the predominant criterion is unforeseeability of the cause of damage. But it is equally true that this criterion has been restrictively interpreted by the courts. This means that unforeseeability is only recognised if the cause of damage lies "outside of the sphere" of the person who has caused the damage.

This principle applies, first of all, in the cases of the liability of the "gardien de la chose" which is, according to Art 1384 s 1 of the Code civil, a strict liability (Cour de Cassation of 30 October 1957). It is interesting to note that this case and others cited in this context are "product liability" cases.

Under German law, "hohere Gewalt" may also be a cause of exoneration even if strict liability applies. But, again, courts admit only those facts which are extraordinary, and - this is the important point - outside the risk which is inherent in the activity under discussion ("betriebsfremd"), for example, a railroad. Only circumstances "coming from outside and caused by the forces of nature" may be taken into consideration, as Larenz says; for example, an unusually heavy snowstorm would be considered, but not sabotage by a mentally sick person blackmailing the railroad.

Applying these principles to product liability, there is no room to pretend that the exclusion of "development risk" is justified by considering the cause of damage, the unavoidable and absolutely undiscoverable defect, to be an Act of God. The cause is inherent in the activity exercised by the producer, the pharmaceutical company in the above mentioned case. It is not "betriebsfremd" or "en dehors du milieu professionel de la personne qui a causé le dommage". No justified distinction can be drawn between the hardly discoverable and the absolutely undiscoverable defect. In both cases, the risk is the same. Liability should, therefore, be extended to this kind of situation which is called "development risk".

## LEGAL HARMONISATION IN EUROPE, PRODUCT LIABILITY A COMPARISON BETWEEN THE DIRECTIVE OF THE EUROPEAN COMMUNITIES AND THE COUNCIL OF EUROPE CONVENTION

*Ferdinando Albanese*
(Deputy Director of Legal Affairs,
Council of Europe)*

1.    Introduction

When  Dean Prosser wrote in 1966 his  famous  article on  "The Fall of the Citadel", nobody could  forecast that  the  European  Citadel  would  resist  so  much longer than the American one.

We thought that the Citadel was going to  surrender  when  in  September 1976 the  Commission  of  the European Communities transmitted to the  Council  of Ministers  a proposal for a Council Directive and  in January  1977 the Council of Europe   "Convention  on Products  Liability in Regard to Personal Injury  and Death"  (hereafter referred to as  "the  Convention") was  opened  to  the  signature  of  member  States. Appendix B, p. 185).

The European  Citadel fell on 25 July  1985  when the Council of Ministers of the European  Communities adopted  the  Directive on the Approximation  of  the Laws,  Regulations and Administrative  Provisions  of the Member States concerning Liability for  Defective Products (hereafter referred to as "the Directive"). (Appendix A, p. 173)

The   existence, at   the European level,   of  two legal instruments raises the question of the  differences  between  the two texts.  If  the  differences exist,  it  should  be  considered whether and  to  what extent the Convention should be made compatible  with the Directive.

---

*     The  views  expressed  in these  pages  are  the author's and not those of the Council of Europe.

In order to take a stand on these questions I propose making a comparison between the two texts under 7 main headings:

(a)  The Basis for Liability

(b)  Persons Liable

(c)  Products Subject to the Regime of Products Liability

(d)  Persons Entitled to Sue

(e)  Defences Allowed to the Producers

(f)  Compensation of Damage

(g)  Duration of the Producer's Liability.

2.  Comparison

(a)  The Basis for Liability. The basis for liability in the two instruments is the same: strict liability for a defect in the product.

Article 1 of the Directive reads: "The producer shall be liable for damage caused by a defect in his product" and Article 3(1) of the Convention: "The producer shall be liable to pay compensation for death or personal injuries caused by a defect in his product".

The definition of "defect", contained in paragraph (c) of Article 2 of the Convention, is rather concise:

"A product has a 'defect' when it does not provide the safety which a person is entitled to expect, having regard to all the circumstances including the presentation of the product".

The definition contained in Article 6 of the Directive is more detailed:

"1.  A product is defective when it does not provide the safety which a person is entitled to expect, taking all circumstances into account, including:

(a)  the presentation of the product;

(b)  the use to which it could reasonably be expected that the product would be put;

(c)    the time  when the product  was  put into
circulation.

2.    A product shall not be considered defective  for the sole reason that a  better  product
is subsequently put into circulation."

From a substantive point of view, no  difference
exists  between the two texts.  The reference to  the
"use" of the product, mentioned in paragraph 1(b)  of
Article  6  of the Directive, merely  makes  explicit
elements  of  the definition of the defect  given  by
the  Convention,  elements  which  are  mentioned  in
paragraph  36  of  the  Explanatory  Report  to  the
Convention which reads:

"In determining whether a defect exists it  will
be  necessary, consequently, to take account  of
all  the circumstances, for example, if the  product  was  utilised more or  less  correctly  or
used  in a more or less foreseeable way (if  the
actions  of  the consumer amount to  fault,  but
the  product  nevertheless  is  regarded  as
defective,  the  situation will be  governed  by
Article  4).  The committee did not,  of  course
wish  to enumerate all these circumstances,  but
it  did expressly indicate one, namely the  presentation  of  the product, so that in  all  the
States  the  notion  of  'defect'  would  cover
incorrect  or incomplete directions for  use  or
warnings.  As  it  is,  the  legislation  or
judicial decisions of some States consider  that
only  'intrinsic' defects are real  defects  and
hold that incomplete or incorrect directions  or
warnings do not amount to 'intrinsic' defects."

The reference to the "time" factor in  paragraph
1(c)  of  Article 6 of the Directive is  also  making
clear a point which is dealt with in paragraph 37  of
the  Explanatory  Report  to  the  Convention  which
emphasises:

"The  question was posed as to whether it  would
not be expedient to stipulate the time at  which
the safety of a product must be determined.   It
was  suggested  that  the  safe  nature  of  the
product  must be judged at the time the  product
was  put  into circulation and not at  the  time
when  the  damage occurred.  The  committee  was
against  including any stipulation of this  kind
in paragraph (c) since it would implicitly  admit
as an exception 'development risks'.   Moreover,
the  definition of 'defect' in paragraph (c) gave
the  judge a sufficient  margin  of  appreciation

to enable him to take the time factor into account."

Paragraph 2 of Article 6 of the Directive, finally, makes explicit the concept of "subsequent defect" which constitutes a ground for exemption from liability also under the Convention as is explained at length in paragraph 42 of the Explanatory Report to the Convention:

"On the other hand the committee agreed that a distinction should be made between 'development risks' and other situations in which the 'time factor' played a part and which were covered by the definition of a 'defect'. This is a case of 'subsequent defects', that is to say defects which were not considered as such when the product was put into circulation but became 'defects', in the meaning of the definition, as the result of new technological discoveries. In other words, the product is manufactured in accordance with the rules in force at the time when it is put into circulation but can no longer be regarded as complying with the rules governing safety following new scientific and technological development. The defect may then be revealed by comparison with a similar product manufactured according to the new methods. It is, for example, obvious that if a person buys in 1977 a refrigerator manufactured in 1948 which lacks certain safety devices (such as a door that can be opened from inside) included in 1977 models, that person is not entitled to expect the same degree of safety as would be offered by a refrigerator manufactured in 1977."

In conclusion, I should like to emphasise two things about the definition of "defect" given by the Directive and the Convention: firstly, it is objective, since it does not refer to the safety which the victim or a particular consumer is entitled to expect and, secondly, it is relative, because safety must be assessed in each case according to the circumstances. I believe that this notion avoids certain abuses which were denounced with regard to American law, since in determining the product's safety it will be necessary to take into account any improper use or inadequate maintenance of the product by the victim.

It follows from these provisions that the producer is liable for a defect in his product, even if he has not committed any fault or been negligent.

That is why the Convention refers to "products liability" and not "producers' liability".

The injured person, for his part, is required to prove the damage, the defect and the causal link between the defect and the damage. I must particularly stress the fact that the plaintiff must prove these elements, which exclude the possibility of a "presumption" by the judge of the existence of the defect. This avoids one of the distortions of American law denounced in the U.S.A. It should be noticed that whereas Article 4 of the Directive states these requirements expressly, it is considered, in Strasbourg, that they were implied in the system set up by the Convention.

The producer can escape liability only by proving one of the circumstances which are mentioned by the Convention as defences. We shall see later what these defences are.

(b) <u>Persons Liable</u>. The two instruments are substantially identical as to the determination of the persons liable. The person principally liable is the manufacturer of the finished product or of a component part and the producer of natural products (the Directive however uses the expression "raw material").

This definition excludes all other persons involved in the production and distribution chain, such as suppliers, warehousers, retailers, who are covered by the Hague Convention on conflicts of law in the field of product liability.

It may be wondered why the Convention and the Directive are aimed at restricting the application of the new liability system to "real" producers. The reason, at least as far as the Convention is concerned, is that it was thought, in Strasbourg, inexpedient and economically costly in terms of legislative policy, to impose strict liability on a large number of persons some of whom play a secondary part in the production process.

The basic thinking behind this is as follows: since we are concerned with products liability, the person responsible must be the one who had the possibility of exercising quality control, who put the product into the state in which it is offered to the public - and which is the origin of the damage suffered by the consumer - and who, through insurance, is able to spread the risk inherent in production over a large number of products.

On the other hand, the producer of a component part is also liable under the Convention and the Directive. I know that this provision has been criticised by those who would have preferred channelling liability entirely on to the producer of the finished product. It must be borne in mind however that strict liability on the part of the producer of a component part is justified not only in terms of principle (the component is in itself a finished product which might be defective), but also in practical terms. Such liability is both in the interests of the consumer, since the component manufacturer may be financially in a better position than the producer of the finished product, and in the interests of the producer of the component part himself, who may not wish to leave the defence of his case to someone else.

However, it was realised that to regard the "real" producer alone as liable might in some cases make consumer protection meaningless since frequently: (i) the real producer is a foreigner and has no office in the victim's country; (ii) the name which appears on the product is not that of the real producer, who often has insufficient financial standing to offer an adequate guarantee to the victim, but is the name of a large store; (iii) the product is "anonymous", that is to say it bears no name, neither that of the manufacturer nor that of the distributor.

Consequently, in order to avoid any loopholes, the Convention and the Directive mention a number of persons who are equally liable with the producer and other persons who have a subsidiary liability.

The persons who have the same liability as the producer are:

(i)     the importer of the product (in the case of the Directive, the importer within the Community),

(ii)    the person presenting the product as his by showing on it his name, his trade mark or other distinctive sign. This applies to products marketed under the name of a large store.

Subsidiary liability is borne by the supplier of the product where the product states the identity neither of the producer nor of the importer and the supplier fails to divulge the identity of the producer or the person who supplied him with the product.

In all cases where several persons are liable
under the Convention or the Directive they are
jointly liable. Each of those persons has a recourse
action against the other but the Strasbourg
Convention, not dealing with this problem, refers
back to national legislation. The reason why we
could not cover this problem in Strasbourg is because
of the membership of the Organisation which comprises
21 Member States between whom there is no agreement
of the type of the Brussels Convention or recognition
and enforcement of judicial decisions. Article 5 of
the Directive makes this explicit by stating "...
without prejudice to the provisions of national law
concerning the right of contribution or recourse".

(c) Products Subject to the Regime of Products
Liability. According to Article 2(a) of the
Convention, the term "product" indicates all movables, natural or industrial, whether raw or manufactured, even though incorporated into another movable or into an immovable. This definition clearly
shows that the Convention applies to all products
except immovables which, in most countries, are
already subject to a special system of liability.

Article 2 of the Directive introduces an important difference since it excludes from the field of
application of the strict liability regime "primary
agricultural products and game" which are defined as
"products of the soil, of stock-farming and of fisheries, excluding products which have undergone
initial processing".

(d) Persons Entitled to Sue. Neither the Directive
nor the Convention contain any provisions specifying
persons entitled to sue. In the absence of a
definition, Article 1 of the Directive and Article
3, paragraph 1 of the Convention are drafted in such
a way as to lead to the conclusion that any injured
person, whether he is party to a contract or not
and whether he is the user of the product or a
bystander, benefits from the strict liability system.

The two instruments supersede therefore the
distinction between "contractual" and "tortious"
liability by simply introducing an additional right
of action (see Article 12 of the Convention and
Article 13 of the Directive) for all victims which
is based on "strict liability". This makes it
possible for the injured person to decide whether to
take action either under the strict liability system
or on the ground of fault or, depending on the
situation in question and on the systems of
municipal law, under the terms of a contract.

Municipal law will be able to regulate the relationship between these different systems of liability as well as any incompatibility between them.

(e) <u>Defences Allowed to the Producers</u>. In a strict liability system, only the defences expressly allowed to the person liable can be used.

The defences that both the Directive and the Convention grant to producers are:

(i)      the product has not been put into circulation by the producer;

(ii)     the defect did not exist at the moment when the product was put into circulation;

(iii)    the producer is not liable if he proves that the product was neither manufactured for sale, hire or any other form of distribution for the economic purposes of the producer nor manufactured or distributed in the course of his business;

(iv)     the contributory negligence of the victim which, having regard to all circumstances, can be a cause for reducing or disallowing compensation.

The Directive addresses three other defences:

(i)      the defect is due to compliance of the product with mandatory regulations issued by the public authorities;

(ii)     the state of scientific and technical knowledge at the time when he [the producer] put the producer into circulation was not such as to enable the existence of the defect to be discovered;

(iii)    in the case of a manufacturer of a component, the defect is attributable to the design of the product in which the component has been fitted or to the instructions given by the manufacturer of the product.

The last of these defences is also provided by the Convention but not in an explicit way. Paragraph 51 of the explanatory report to the Convention reads:

"The committee considered that there was no
need for the Convention to contain a provision
enabling the producer of the component part to
establish that he is not liable by proving that
the defect resulted from the design or instructions of the producer of the product into which
it was incorporated.

The reason is that it follows from Article 3,
paragraph 1, taken together with Article 2,
paragraph (b), that the producer of a component
part is liable only if that component part is
defective, and this is for the injured party to
demonstrate and prove. The point about the
question of defectiveness, according to Article
2, paragraph (c), is whether the component part
considered in itself – that is, as an autono-
mous product – does not provide the safety that
may legitimately be expected of it.

If the component part in itself satisfies legitimate safety requirements, the liability of
the producer of that part cannot be invoked.
This principle applies even if the finished product as a whole is defective because the component part, owing to the general design of the
producer of the finished product, was unsuitable for incorporation into that finished product, and also if the component part was manufactured according to technical specifications
provided by the manufacturer of the finished
product and it then transpires that those
specifications were erroneous. Article 3,
paragraph 4, does not apply in such cases.

If on the other hand, the component part, considered as an independent product – that is,
without regard to its subsequent use by the
manufacturer of the finished product – does not
meet the safety requirements that may legitimately be expected of it, then the producer of
that component part is liable, under Article 3,
paragraph 1, taken together with Article 2,
paragraphs (b) and (c)."

The other two defences, that is to say the compliance with national mandatory regulations and the
development risk, constitute an important difference
between the Convention and the Directive.

A defence based on compliance with mandatory
regulations is excluded, in the framework of the Convention, by the use, in the definition of defect, of
the word "entitled" ("safety which a person is

entitled to expect"). Paragraph 35 of the Explanatory Report to the Convention specifies "the word 'entitled' is more general than the word 'legally' [entitled]; in other words, mere observance of statutory rules and rules imposed by authorities does not preclude liability".

The Convention excludes development risk as an exception to the liability of the producer by simply not mentioning it as a defence. Therefore, by virtue of the principle that in a "strict liability" system only the defences which are expressly provided for may be admitted, development risk – which is not mentioned expressly by the Convention as an exception – cannot be accepted as such.

It is interesting to recall the reasons which led the experts in Strasbourg to exclude development risk as a possible defence. The Explanatory Report to the Convention (paragraphs 39, 40 and 41) states:

"Some experts maintained that 'development risks' should be a ground for exclusion of liability in the case of technically advanced products. Any stipulations to the contrary might discourage scientific research and the marketing of new products.

Against this opinion it was argued that such an exception would make the Convention nugatory since it would reintroduce into the system of liability established by the Convention the possibility for the producer to prove the absence of any fault on his part. Exclusion of liability in cases of 'development risk' would also invite the use of the consumer as a 'guinea-pig'.

In conclusion the committee considered that the problem was one of social policy, the main question being whether such risks should be borne by the consumer or the producer and/or, in whole or in part, by the community.

The committee considered that, as insurance made it possible to spread the risk over a large number of products, producers' liability, even for development risks, should not be a serious obstacle to planning and putting into circulation new and useful products.

The committee therefore decided that development risk should not constitute an exception to producers' liability".

It should however be pointed out that even in the framework of the Directive, development risk can be excluded as a defence to the producer. Article 15(b) of the Directive gives to the States the possibility, by way of derogation from Article 7(e), of providing in their legislation that the producer will be liable even in case of development risk.

However, such a derogation is subject to a special procedure which is specified in paragraph 2 of Article 15. A Member State wishing to introduce the exclusion of development risk as a defence, shall communicate the text of the proposed measure to the Commission. The Commission shall inform the other Member States thereof. The Member States concerned shall hold the proposed measures in abeyance for nine months after the Commission is informed and provided that in the meantime the Commission has not submitted to the Council a proposal amending the Directive on the relevant matter. However, if within three months of receiving the said information, the Commission does not advise the Member State concerned that it intends submitting such a proposal to the Council, the Member State may take the proposed measure immediately. If the Commission does submit to the Council such a proposal amending the Directive within the aforementioned nine months, the Member State concerned shall hold the proposed measures in abeyance for a further period of 18 months from the date on which the proposal is submitted.

At any rate, ten years after the date of notification of the Directive, the Commission shall submit to the Council a report on the effect that rulings by the courts as to the application of Article 7(e) (development risk) and of paragraph 1(b) of Article 15 (special procedure to which is subject the exclusion of development risk as a defence) have on consumer protection and the functioning of the Common Market. In the light of this report the Council, acting on a proposal from the Commission and pursuant to the terms of Article 100 of the Treaty, shall decide whether to repeal Article 7(e).

Finally, the producer cannot exclude or limit his liability by any exemption or exoneration clause (Article 8 of the Convention and Article 12 of the Directive).

(f) Compensation of Damage. The next question to be considered is what damage confers entitlement to compensation under the Convention and the Directive.

As the title of the Convention indicates, its application is confined to physical injury and death. The reason why the Council of Europe experts decided on this restriction was that they realised, on the one hand, the urgency of dealing first with the problem of physical injury and, on the other hand, that the problems of liability for damage to property were slightly different and perhaps required a different solution. The Convention does not stipulate heads of damage or forms of compensation, which will accordingly be governed by national law.

The Convention does not provide for any financial limit on liability. However, as in some states the introduction of strict liability has always been accompanied by a restriction on the amount of compensation, the Convention, in order to facilitate ratification by the largest possible number of states, does provide for the possibility of a reservation whereby states will be able to limit the financial extent of the producers' liability, first by an individual claim limit and second by a global limit, provided that the limits are not lower than those stipulated in the Appendix to the Convention.

The Directive covers also (see Article 9, paragraph (b) damage to, or destruction of, any item of property other than the defective product itself, with a lower threshold of 500 ECU provided that the item of property:

> (i) is of a type ordinarily intended for private use or consumption, and

> (ii) was used by the injured person mainly for his own private use or consumption.

The Directive specifies that its Article 9 does not prejudice national provisions relating to non-material damage.

The Directive provides for the possibility of limiting to an amount, which may not be less than 70 million ECU, the total liability for damage resulting from death or personal injury and caused by identical items with the same defect.

Ten years after the date of notification of the Directive, the Commission shall submit to the Council a report on the effect on consumer protection and the functioning of the Common Market of the implementation of the financial limit on liability by those Member States which have used the option.

In the light of this report the Council, acting on a proposal from the Commission and pursuant to the terms of Article 100 of the Treaty, shall decide whether to repeal the financial limit on liabilities.

(g) Duration of the Producer's Liability. Both the Directive and the Convention provide for a ten-year "cut-off", period after which proceedings against a producer cannot be instituted. This "cut-off" period was decided upon in order to preserve a balance between the interests of consumers and producers.

Two arguments were made in Strasbourg to justify such a provision: (i) the necessity to afford producers some security by avoiding their being held liable for damage resulting from a cause which manifests itself after a long period of time; and (ii) the desirability of facilitating insurance and amortisation by fixing a time-limit to the liability.

A difference exists between the Convention and the Directive in this field in so far as Article 11 of the Directive states that actions for damages may not be brought after the expiry of a period of 10 years "unless the injured person has in the meantime instigated proceedings". This is not a substantive difference, I think, because Article 11 only makes explicit a principle emerging from a combination of Article 6 and 7 of the Convention.

The Convention and the Directive provide also for a three-year period of limitation which runs from the day when the injured person became aware or should reasonably have become aware of the damage, the defect and the identity of the producer. The reason why such a provision was introduced into the two instruments is essentially to avoid forum shopping, which might be the consequence of the existence of different limitation periods in different states, some of which would apply the *lex fori* while others would apply *lex causae*.

The Directive adds an element which is not mentioned in the Convention. Paragraph 2 of Article 10 states that "the laws of Member States regulating suspension or interruption of the limitation period shall not be affected by this Directive". This is not a substantive difference between the two texts because the experts of the Council of Europe thought that the principle contained in paragraph 2 of Article 10 of the Directive was a principle generally recognised in this field and therefore applicable to the Convention even without making it explicit.

3.    Conclusions

In conclusion, we may state that there are three important differences of substance between the Directive and the Convention, namely:

(i)     Whereas Article 2 of the Directive states that "'product' means all movables, with the exception of primary agricultural products and game", Article 2(a) of the Convention does apply to these products;

(ii)    Whereas Article 7(d) of the Directive states that the producer shall not be liable when "the defect is due to compliance of the product with mandatory regulations issued by the public authorities", the Convention does not contain this ground for exemption;

(iii)   Whereas Article 7(e) of the Directive exempts the producer from liability when "the state of scientific and technical knowledge at the time when he put the product into circulation was not such as to enable the existence of the defect to be discovered", this ground for exemption, called "development risk", is not provided for in the Convention.

However, it should be noted that the grounds for exemption from producer liability referred to in (i) and (iii) above are in reality optional.

Article 15 of the Directive permits Member States, by a special procedure in the case of "development risk", not to apply the grounds for exemption contained in Article 2 (agricultural products) and in Article 7(e) (development risk). Consequently, those EEC states which chose not to apply these grounds could in theory ratify the Convention while at the same time applying the Directive, whereas the others could not.

On the other hand, ground for exemption based on "conformity with current regulations" (see (ii) above) is mandatory and constitutes the real obstacle to ratification of the Convention by any EEC states which choose not to apply the optional grounds contained in Article 2 and Article 7(e) of the Directive.

Therefore, if it was decided to make the two texts compatible, as I believe is a necessity, a Protocol; amending the Convention should be drawn up. Such a Protocol could either:

(i)     merely insert "conformity with current regulations" as an additional ground for exemption from liability (Article 7(d) of the Directive): or

(ii)    bring the Convention completely into line with the Directive by adding, in addition to the ground for exemption mentioned in (i) above, the two other optional grounds. viz. "primary agricultural products and game" (Article 2 of the Directive) and "development risk" (Article 7(e) of the Directive).

I personally am of the opinion that whereas it is necessary to include in the Convention the ground for exemption provided for in Article 7(d) of the Directive, the inclusion of the other two grounds ("development risk" and "primary agricultural products and game"), these exceptions being facultative, is not a legal necessity but must be the result of a policy decision, taking into account the final position on the Directive taken by the Communities' Member States.

The reason for this is that if a group of EEC Member States were to choose not to apply these last two grounds, they could also ratify the Convention which would thus afford a higher degree of consumer protection than that provided for in the Directive.

Thus the Convention would become a long-term objective for those states which are at present able to accept only the level of protection offered by the Directive and its optional grounds for exemption and would like to see the result of the implementation of the Convention and the Directive without its optional grounds before deciding whether to increase consumer protection and ratify the Convention.

In this respect it should be noted that, under the terms of the Directive itself, 10 years after its date of notification the Commission is required to submit to the Council a report on the effect on consumer protection and on the functioning of the Common Market of the absence or presence of "risk development" as a ground for exemption in Member States' legislation. It is not therefore excluded that the Commission, in the light of such a report, might be induced to propose repealing "development risk" as a defence for the producer.

The modification of the Council of Europe Convention, although necessary, may not occur in the near future. In fact, the Directive gives to the Member States a period of three years, from the date of notification of the Directive, for bringing into force the laws, regulations and administrative provisions necessary to comply with the Directive. It can therefore be imagined that the EEC Member States may not take a decision on whether to avail themselves of the options provided by Articles 2 and 7(e), before the expiry of such a period of three years.

We can then conclude that if the European Citadel has fallen, its walls have not yet actually been destroyed and we still do not know whether some pieces of them will persist.

Aubrey L. Diamond

# PRODUCT LIABILITY: COMPENSATION FOR DEATH AND PERSONAL INJURY IN ENGLISH LAW

*Aubrey L. Diamond*

Since 1932 the principles governing liability for death or personal injury caused by defective products have not changed in the law of England and Wales. The pattern of strict liability in contract was established in the nineteenth century, and liability for negligence owes its present form to a famous decision of 1932.

## 1. Strict Liability

In this paper "strict liability" is used to mean liability irrespective of fault. There may or may not be fault or negligence, but that is irrelevant: the defendant is liable even if no fault is shown by the plaintiff, even if the defendant shows that he took reasonable care and even if no amount of care by the defendant could have prevented the plaintiff's injury or loss.

Where there is a direct contractual relationship between the plaintiff and the defendant, the defendant is liable to the plaintiff for loss caused by the defendant's breach of contract. The contractual promise by the defendant need not necessarily give rise to strict liability. If the contract requires the defendant to take reasonable care and no more, then one may talk of contractual liability for negligence.[1] We will see an example of this shortly. But if the contract contains a promise by the defendant that something specific will be done or that a specified state of affairs will exist, whether or not it is within the defendant's control, there will be a breach of contract if that something is not

---

\* For footnotes see p. 43

done or if that state of affairs does not come about. This is a strict liability, for the absence of fault is irrelevant.

For example, in *Dodd and Dodd v Wilson and McWilliiam*[2] the defendant veterinary surgeons inoculated the plaintiffs' cows against summer mastitis. There was something wrong with the toxoid, which caused a serious outbreak of sickness in the cattle. The toxoid was obtained by the defendants from chemists and there was no way they could have detected the defect. The chemists were also innocent of fault, for they had obtained it from the manufacturing laboratories which had made it. No allegations of negligence were made against the defendants and the judge said that "no one concerned in this case has made the slightest imputation with regard to anything which they did." Nevertheless, they were held liable for breach of the term implied at common law in contracts for work and materials that the materials supplied under the contract would be reasonably fit for the purpose for which they were used.[3] They were, of course, entitled to be indemnified by the chemists who in turn received an indemnity from the manufacturers.

So, too, in *Ashington Piggeries Ltd. v Christopher Hill Ltd.*[4] a food for mink which contained herring meal was toxic. It "was no one's fault", said Lord Diplock. "In the then state of knowledge, scientific and commercial, no deliberate exercise of human skill or judgment could have prevented the meal from having its toxic effect on mink. It was sheer bad luck." Despite this, the sellers were liable to the buyers, in the unanimous view of the House of Lords, because the food was not reasonably fit for its known purpose in breach of the implied condition of fitness for purpose in section 14 of the Sale of Goods Act 1893 (now re-enacted in the Sale of Goods Act 1979). It is clear from this case that it is no defence to this strict liability that the goods are as safe as the "state of the art" will allow.

Both the cases just referred to, although involving injury to living creatures, were cases of damage to property resulting from a defect in the goods supplied. But no distinction of principle is drawn in the United Kingdom between damage to property and injury to human beings.[5] (There are however different periods of limitation prescribed.) If a breach of the contractual obligations as to the quality or fitness for purpose of goods leads to death or personal injury, liability to compensate

arises in the same way. In the main, this paper will
concentrate on death or personal injury.

## 2.  Negligence

Where there is no contract between the plaintiff and
the defendant, the plaintiff cannot rely on the
strict contractual liability even if there is a contract with someone else. In English law there is as
yet no *jus quaesitum tertio*. The plaintiff must in
these circumstances base a claim on negligence - that
is, on breach of a duty to take reasonable care. If
the defendant could not have foreseen what went
wrong, or if the accident occurred despite the
defendant's reasonable care, there will be no liability.

Thus when Mr. Steer bought a hot-water bottle
which was defective and which scalded his six-year-
old daughter, she herself could not sue the seller of
the hot-water bottle claiming a breach of the Sale of
Goods Act on the ground that it was not fit for its
purpose. She had not bought the article. Her action
was against the manufacturer and was founded on an
allegation of negligence.[6] In the same way, a wife
cannot sue on the contract of sale if her husband was
the buyer[7] and a person cannot sue on the contract of
sale if the goods were bought by a friend.[8]

It is not necessary here to examine the law of
negligence in detail. It will suffice to quote the
well-known words of Lord Atkin, where in very modern
terminology he refers to manufactured goods as "products" and to the "consumer": ".... a manufacturer of
products, which he sells in such a form as to show
that he intends them to reach the ultimate consumer
in the form in which they left him with no reasonable
possibility of intermediate examination, and with the
knowledge that the absence of reasonable care ...
will result in injury to the consumer's life or
property, owes a duty to the consumer to take that
reasonable care."[9]

No procedural difficulties arise where the same
facts give rise to a claim in tort (for example,
negligence) and a claim in contract. The plaintiff
can choose which cause of action to rely upon and,
indeed, can in appropriate cases rely on both causes
of action if they are not inconsistent, though he can
of course be compensated only once.

## 3.  Reform Proposals

It is the difference between the legal rights of the

contracting buyer and those of other persons injured that has given rise to proposals to reform the law so as to remove the anomalies. In the United Kingdom the proposal that the injured person, whether or not he is a party to a contract, should have a direct right of action against the manufacturer, with the benefit of strict liability, has been made in a joint report of the Law Commission and the Scottish Law Commission[10] and by the Royal Commission on Civil Liability and Compensation for Personal Injury under the chairmanship of the late Lord Pearson.[11] In Europe the European Convention on Products Liability in regard to Personal Injury and Death was promulgated in 1977, and the European Commission's original proposal for a Council Directive relating to the approximation of the laws, regulations and administrative provisions of the Member States concerning liability for defective products was presented in September 1976 and came to fruition with the making of the Directive on 25 July 1985.

These proposals have raised a number of issues that have proved to be controversial, and although in one sense the provisions of the Directive have settled the policy decisions it will still be worth looking at some of these questions after first considering some of the practical differences.

4.   Differences?

Although the nature of strict contractual liability clearly differs in juristic terms from liability for negligence, we must consider how much difference the implementation of the Directive will make when it introduces strict liability as against the manufacturer. The likely answer is: Not very much.

Consider the case of *Hill v J. Crowe (Cases) Ltd.*[12] The defendants manufactured wooden packing cases. The plaintiff, a lorry driver, was sent to pick up a load of goods which had been packed in cases manufactured by the defendants. When the cases of goods completely covered the floor of the lorry he started to stack a second layer of goods on top of them. To do this he had to stand on one of the packing cases. While doing so the case stove in; he fell, and was injured.

It is hardly necessary to point out that he was not in any contractual relationship with the defendants, and nor were his employers. It is however instructive to consider what his position would have been had he been the actual buyer of the packing case that collapsed under his weight. To claim damages he would have to bring his claim under section 14(3) of the Sale of Goods Act (fitness for a particular purpose) or section 14(2) (merchantable quality). It is unlikely that he would, as buyer, have expressly stated that he wanted to stand on the packing case, so any claim under section 14(3) of the Act on the ground that there was a breach of the implied term that the case was fit for a particular purpose would have depended on the making known of that purpose by implication. This would depend on the same facts as need to be shown to rely on a breach of the implied term of merchantability under section 14(2) - that it was not fit for its usual purposes. We can therefore consider the possible application of section 14(2).

Could the plaintiff as hypothetical buyer have shown that the implied term of merchantable quality required the case to be strong enough to be used for the purpose of standing on? The evidence needed to prove this would have been as to the usual or common purposes to which such packing cases are put. A moment's thought will show that this would be the same evidence as would be needed in a negligence action to show that the manufacturers should have foreseen the use to which the product would be put. Thus the theoretical strict liability of proceedings based on the contract of sale would have boiled down to the same issues and same evidence as the actual proceedings based on negligence.

In fact, when the case was tried this caused no problem. The defendants' own evidence was that the cases should be capable of bearing the weight of four men and that there had been no previous complaint similar to the instant one. Their account of the high standards of workmanship and supervision in their factory persuaded the judge that the accident in this case could not have happened unless something had gone wrong, and that the negligence of an employee, for which the defendants would be vicariously liable, was the probable cause. The plaintiff accordingly succeeded in his negligence claim.

A study of the American cases decided on the principle of strict liability also demonstrates that strict liability does not eliminate questions of foreseeability. It is probably not going too far to say that many of the American strict liability cases would have been decided in the same way in England on the basis of negligence.

If all this is correct, then what is the fuss about? Why is the policy of strict liability embodied in the EEC Directive still controversial? Why oppose a regime of strict liability to replace one based on negligence? Or, at an earlier stage, why propose a move from negligence to strict liability? The answer is, of course, that although the different bases of liability would make no difference in many cases, there are some cases - perhaps only a few - where they would make a difference, and it is the treatment of those cases that is important if irrational anomalies are to be removed from the law.

One such case is where someone has been negligent for whom the defendant is not vicariously liable. The decision cited earlier involving veterinary surgeons who inoculated cows is perhaps an example.[13] Another case is where the risk was unknown and, perhaps, unknowable to the defendant, or where all the care and skill in the world could not have prevented the injury - the "state of the art" or development risk cases. *Ashington Piggeries Ltd. v Christopher Hill Ltd.*[14] is such a case, as is *Frost v Aylesbury Dairy Co.*[15] where the dairy claimed that they had done everything possible in the then state of medical and scientific knowledge to supply pure milk but were nevertheless held liable for the death of the plaintiff's wife by typhoid fever caused by their milk. These cases can be contrasted with a well-known negligence case, *Roe v Minister of Health*[16] where the plaintiffs were seriously injured by a contaminated spinal anaesthetic some years before the first publication which described the risk of storing the glass ampoules containing the anaesthetic in a solution of phenol. It was held that there was no negligence and thus no liability.

The shades of meaning being discussed here match those canvassed by the Law Commission in their working paper on implied terms in contracts for the supply of goods,[17] where they distinguished between a term that the supplier would take reasonable care (that is, liability for negligence), a term that the goods would be as fit as care and skill could make them (that is, a promise that no one had been negligent), and a term that the goods would be fit (that is, strict liability).

In theory it is for the plaintiff to prove his case, and in order to do so he must prove every fact on which his case depends. In a case based on strict liability his task is not too difficult. He must prove the contract and its terms (in a case brought under the Sale of Goods Act), the breach of contract or the defect in the goods, the injury, and causation - the link between the defect and the injury. Causation may well be the most difficult matter to

show.   In   a   negligence case, the plaintiff's task
looks  more difficult, since he must call evidence to
satisfy  the court that the defendant, or someone for
whom the defendant is responsible, has failed to take
reasonable care.  On the face of it, the plaintiff is
at  a disadvantage.  He knows little or nothing about
the   manufacturing   process,   and   there   are clearly
major problems in trying to trace what happened to an
individual  item on its way through the manufacturing
process  months  or,  perhaps,  years before.  But in
practice   there   are many cases where this is not too
difficult.   If the plaintiff proves that the product
which   injured   him   was   defective   and that this is
something  which  does  not  or should not ordinarily
happen,   the   burden   will   shift to the defendant to
show   that   the defect occurred without negligence on
his   part.   This is what happened in *Steer v Durable
Rubber  Manufacturing  Co.  Ltd.*[18]  and  in *Hill v J.
Crowe  (Cases)  Ltd.*[19],  in  both  of which cases the
manufacturers'  assertions  that  standards were high
and that such a defect had not occurred before helped
to  persuade  the  court  that  there  must have been
negligence in the instant case.

A   practical difference between cases founded on
strict   liability and those founded on negligence may
be psychological: a manufacturer proud of his reputation   naturally   resents   an allegation of negligence
and  may  well  fight  the  case  to refute the slur.
There  is no such slur if the case is based on strict
liability.    It   would be interesting to conduct research   to   see   whether   it is more common to settle
claims  of  one kind rather tha another.  Against the
theory that negligence cases are harder to settle, it
may be noted that most cases are handled by insurers,
that  where reputation is known to be at stake, as in
professional  negligence policies, it is the practice
to  include  a "Q.C. clause" in the insurance policy,
and  that  the  Q.C. clause is designed to facilitate
settlements   out   of   court   without any admission or
finding  of liability in order to avoid the publicity
of a trial.

## 5.   Types of Goods

One  of  the  controversial  issues  in discussing
reforms,  and  one  on which the EEC Directive allows
Member  States  some  discretion[20],  is whether strict
liability  should  apply  to  all  types of goods, or
whether  some  should  be excluded from the regime or
treated in some special way.

(a)  All Goods.  A strong argument for including all
goods  within  a  strict  liability regime is that the

present law, a combination of negligence and strict liability as we have seen, does not distinguish between different types of goods. Nevertheless, various particular types of goods have been suggested as apppropriate for special rules or for exclusion from the universal regime.

(b) Natural Products. Article 2 of the Directive of 25 July 1985 defines "product" as meaning all movables "with the exception of primary agricultural products and game". "Game" is not defined and will have its ordinary dictionary meaning of wild animals and birds hunted for sport or food. "Primary agricultural products" is not a term that has a precise meaning in English and accordingly has a definition in Article 2: it means "the products of the soil, of stock-farming and of fisheries, excluding products which have undergone initial processing". Member States will however have the option of deleting this exclusion and including primary agricultural products within the strict liability regime of the Directive: Article 15.1(a).

It is not yet known whether the United Kingdom will exercise this option. The two Law Commissions differed in their views on the way natural products should be treated by the law.

The Scottish Law Commission thought that the arguments for strict liability either did not apply, or applied with considerably less force, to "the products of the agricultural and fishing industries in which no process designed to preserve the product or to transform it into a different product has been applied". They recommended that consideration should be given to the exclusion of producers of primary agricultural and fishery products from the regime of strict liability, and Article 2 of the Directive closely follows this.

The Law Commission (for England and Wales), on the other hand, thought that no valid distinction could be made between natural products and other products. The line between natural products and industrial products could not, they said, be drawn with precision and they were clear that coal, stone, minerals and chemicals which are mined, quarried or otherwise obtained from sea or land should be treated in the same way as manufactured goods. This argument has been accepted in the Directive because although these substances may be said to be "products of the soil" they are plainly not "agricultural products". The Law Commission conceded that a distinction could possibly be drawn between foodstuffs which have been

processed and the primary produce of agriculture and
fishing, but even there most food is subject to some
kind of process: "Wheat is made into flour, flour is
made into bread; pigs are made into pork, or bacon,
pork is made into pork pies.    Fruit is tinned;
vegetables are frozen.  Herrings are kippered, plaice
is filleted .... even fresh vegetables .... may have
been sprayed by chemicals and the land in which they
grew artificially fertilised".   Again, some of these
points have been taken note of in the Directive.
Flour is clearly not a primary agricultural product
because it has undoubtedly undergone "processing",
whatever that word may mean.  Has wheat undergone
processing in removing the grains from the stalk and
separating the wheat from the chaff?  Has raw meat in
a butcher's shop undergone processing?  The canning
of fruit certainly involves processing, but what of
frozen vegetables?  It is probable that the fertilis-
ing of land and the spraying of chemicals on fruit
and vegetables would not be regarded as "initial
processing", but the consequences for the consumer
may nevertheless be serious.  Perhaps the chickens
produced by what is widely known as "factory farming"
would be regarded as primary agricultural products,
though there is of course room for argument whether
plucking, the removal of internal organs and packing
are to be regarded as processing.

The doubts may offer strong reasons why no such
exclusion from the scope of the new law should be
made, though one might always say that the ultimate
drawing of lines would be a matter for the courts.
It is not irrelevant that there is no exemption from
the strict liability under the Sale of Goods Act in
respect of any such products (no doubt the milk in
*Frost v Aylesbury Dairy Co.*[21] would be regarded as
having been processed), so if a purpose of the exclusion is to protect the poor little farmer from
liability it may be noted that the poor little green-
grocer or fishmonger is already strictly liable to a
buyer, and can make the farmer or fisherman liable
down the contractual chain.  That, of course, depends
on whether the particular farmer or fisherman (or,
more likely, fishery company) can be traced.  That
very problem is addressed in the Directive, for
Article 3.3 provides that where the producer of the
product cannot be identified, each supplier of the
product is to be treated as its producer.

(c) <u>Components</u>.    A manufacturer makes a product.
That product is then used by another manufacturer in
making another product.  The component may have no
independent use apart from its use in another product, such as a nut or a car headlamp, or it may be an

independent product in its own right though used in
this case as a component, such as a cushion supplied
as part of an armchair.[22]

As with natural products, problems of definition
arise which are not solved by simply talking about
"components". The Directive does not offer a
definition. In Article 1 "product" is defined as
meaning all movables "even though incorporated into
another movable", and in Article 2.1 "producer" includes the producer of any raw material or the manufacturer of a component part. One of the defences
specifically provided by Article 7 applies in the
case of a manufacturer of a component: by paragraph
(f) he is not liable if he proves that the defect is
attributable to the design of the product in which
the component has been fitted or to the instructions
given by the manufacturer of the product.

The word "fitted" may be noted. Is it necessary
that a component should be fixed to the finished
product by screwing, glueing or in some other way, or
can it be simply placed in position? Are a plastic
cup and saucer placed with other articles into a box
called a "picnic set" components of the finished
picnic set? Is an ice tray a component of a
refrigerator? Are tyres components of the finished
car? If not, why not? Sometimes it is not easy to
say which is the component and which the finished
product. In the case of the car, presumably both the
complete car without tyres and the separate tyres are
"components" of the car with tyres, but what of a
complete television set handed to a skilled carpenter
to construct a cabinet for the television, which ends
up as a television in a wooden cabinet. Is the
television set a "component" of the finished product
produced by the carpenter (who would then be strictly
liable as the producer of the finished product), or
is the wooden cabinet a "component" of the television
set? Is the order of events the main determinant or
are we (as seems more sensible) to look at the
substance of what has taken place?

(d) Pharmaceutical Products. Drugs are a special
case, for several reasons. One is that the possibility of a really large scale disaster, with thousands,
even tens of thousands, of victims exists as it does
for perhaps no other goods. Another is the inherent
capacity to harm. Reactions to the same drug can
vary so much from individual to individual that the
element of unpredictability looms larger here than
anywhere else. Indeed, in a sense anything is
foreseeable.

I have dealt elsewhere with the problems that arise in the development and marketing of drugs, and expressed my personal belief that this is one area where a "no-fault" scheme is worth exploring.[23] Under a "no-fault" scheme claims would be made against a separately administered fund and not against an individual manufacturer (though the scheme could provide for the right of the fund to claim an indemnity from an individual manufacturer in special circumstances).

## 6.  State of the Art

The discussion of the two related ideas of "state of the art" and "development risk" as possible defences to a claim in product liability has been made difficult by the absence of any precise notion of what these expressions encompass. The Pearson Commission[24] referred to "the 'state of the art' defence available under the present system of liability in negligence", and a common criticism of such a defence is that it reduces so-called strict liability to negligence liability. We now know what is meant in the EEC context, for Article 7(e) lays down that the producer is not liable if he proves "that the state of scientific and technical knowledge at the time when he put the product into circulation was not such as to enable the existence of the defect to be discovered". This seem to be a narrow defence, for there is no geographical or economic limit to the words "knowledge" and "enable". Presumably the state of scientific knowledge at the time of manufacture is a question of fact, but it is to be noted that the paragraph does not restrict the knowledge to be taken into account to that available to the producer. He must be taken to have access to the world's libraries and computers, in all probability. Similarly the expense of ensuring safety would not entitle the producer to claim that he was unable to discover the defect, and the Directive does not permit him to claim that a discoverable defect could not have been prevented.

At the same time the Directive does provide that in determining whether a product is defective – whether it provides the safety which a person is entitled to expect – all the circumstances must be taken into account, including the time when the product was put into circulation: Article 6.1. In addition Article 6.2 states that a product is not to be considered defective "for the sole reason that a better product is subsequently put into circulation".

The relations between the state of the art defence, the provisions of Article 6, negligence and

strict liability are complex and difficult and no
doubt we shall have to wait for case law to understand them fully. Is a car sold without seat belts
defective? It would be today, but not, it seems, if
it was put into circulation before seat belts were
generally installed. At one time refrigerators
generally had doors which locked shut until an external catch was operated. Several children died after
crawling inside because the door could not be pushed
open from inside. Today all refrigerators have
magnetic catches which can be opened from inside.
Would one with an old-style lock be regarded as
defective today? It would be hard to say that at the
time it was put into circulation the state of knowledge was not such as to enable the existence of the
defect to be discovered - a few minutes' thought
might cause a manufacturer to visualise the
possibility of a tragedy - but at the time it was put
into circulation the risk would not have been
regarded as one it was necessary to guard against, so
that it may be that the product was not then
defective.

    How would the state of the art defence operate
in the thalidomide case? Throughout the litigation
and agitation the manufacturers denied negligence,
and perhaps they would have been able to show that in
the state of scientific knowledge at the time when
the drug was put into circulation (it is thought that
this refers to the actual tablet that injured the
victim and not the first putting into circulation of
the drug) the existence of the defect could not have
been discovered. It would, I think, have been
impossible for them to argue under Article 6 that at
that time it would have been regarded as safe.
Nevertheless it is certainly on the cards that the
state of the art defence would have protected the
manufacturer. This must be regarded as something of
a paradox, for undoubtedly the thalidomide tragedy
gave a great impetus to the world-wide movement for
strict liability.

7.   Conclusion

New legislation never solves all the problems, and
often raises new problems that did not exist in the
old law. The Directive on liability for defective
products will be no exception. It is still too early
to discuss the problems it will raise, for much will
depend on the way it is implemented. If it is
translated into a whole new British statute, a
permissible way of implementing a Directive, we shall
have to wait to see the actual words used.

Of one thing one can be reasonably sure. The passing of the necessary legislation will alert both the public and the legal profession to the existence of remedies for injuries caused by defective products. Not all claims will succeed, but there will be more claims made. This probability will lead to increased insurance premiums in the early years Claims experience may well show that the overall level of compensation is not such as to justify the increases. But by then inflation will have caught up, and premiums are unlikely to go down again. The price, spread over consumers at large, is unlikely to be great, and will be worth paying to eliminate the anomalies in the present law.

## FOOTNOTES

1    See, for example, Unfair Contract Terms Act 1977, s 1.

2    [1946] 2 All ER 691, KBD.

3    See now Supply of Goods and Services Act 1982, s 1(5).

4    [1972] AC 441; [1971] 1 All ER 847, HL.

5    See, for example, *Frost v Aylesbury Dairy Co* [1905] 1 KB 608, CA.

6    *Steer v Durable Rubber Manufacturing Co Ltd., The Times*, 20 November 1958, CA. She succeeded.

7    *Heill v Hedges* [1951] 1 TLR 512, KBD; *Daniels and Daniels v R. White & Sons Ltd* [1938] 4 All ER 258, KBD.

8    *Donoghue v Stevenson* [1932] AC 562, HL.

9    *Ibid* at p 599.

10   Report on Liability for Defective Products, Law Com No 82, Scot Law Com No 45, Cmnd 6831 (1977).

11   Cmnd 7054 (1978).

12   [1978] 1 All ER 812, QBD.

13   *Dodd v Wilson* [1946] 2 All ER 691, n.2 supra.

14   [1972] AC 441, n.4 supra.

15   [1905] 1 KB 608, CA.

16   [1954] 2 QB, 66, CA.

17   Law Commission, Working Paper No 71 (1977), para 49.

18   *The Times*, 20 November 1958, n 6, supra.

19   [1978] 1 All ER 812, n 12, supra.

20   Directive, Articles 2, 3 and 15.1(a).

21   [1905] 1 KB 608, CA.

22   Lest it be asked what product liability has to do with cushions, it ought to be pointed out that deaths have been caused by toxic fumes given off by inflammable upholstery.

23   *Consumer Law in the EEC*, ed Woodroffe (Sweet and Maxwell, 1984), chapter IX, "Product Liability and Pharmaceuticals in the United Kingdom".

24   Cmnd 7054 (1978), para 1258.

## ECONOMIC LOSS AND PRODUCTS LIABILITY

*Peter Cane*

### 1.  Preliminary Points

In 1979 I published an article[1][*] in which I attempted
to state  the rules governing the liability of manufacturers  and builders in tort for economic loss and
property damage resulting from negligence in the making and  marketing of products and buildings.  There
have been  significant developments in the law since
that article was written and this paper will be a
partial  restatement  taking  account  of  those
developments.

A  number  of  the  principles which I stated in
that article were derived from cases dealing with
defective premises rather than defective products.  I
expressed the view that the principles could be
applied,  *mutatis mutandis*, as much to products as to
premises and I see no reason to change that view.  It
is true, of course, that vendors and lessors have
traditionally enjoyed some immunity from liability in
negligence in respect of the state of premises but
this immunity does not exist where the vendor or
lessor is also the builder.[2]  Furthermore, the
distinction between products and premises is an artificial one, in that in some cases at least, of which
*Junior Books Ltd v Veitchi Co Ltd*[3] is an example, the
cause of complaint is some separately identifiable
component of the building rather than the way in
which or the location at which the components were
put together.  The transformation of chattels into
fixtures is relevant to the law of property but not
to the law of torts.  The reason why so many of the
leading cases concern buildings may be that defects
in buildings are more likely to cause economic loss
of a magnitude worth litigating about than are

---

[*]    For footnotes see p.68

defects in products. It may be, too, that the
problem of latency of damage, which I will discuss in
due course, is likely to be greater in building
cases, and this would explain why the recent cases on
limitation of actions[4] have concerning buildings
rather than products.

Another issue I skated over in the earlier
article was the importance of the fact that in all
the building cases up till then the property itself
had suffered some physical damage or deterioration as
a result of the defendant's negligence. This fortuitous circumstance enabled the courts to avoid
head-on consideration of liability for purely economic loss consisting either of the cost of simply
remedying a defect or of loss consequential on a pure
defect of quality. The law now appears to be in a
somewhat confused state in this respect. On the one
hand, *Junior Books v Veitchi*[5] would appear to justify
the assertion that economic loss consisting of the
cost of remedying a defect, or of loss consequential
on a pure defect of quality,[6] is recoverable, at
least in some cases, regardless of the fact that the
defect has not caused, and is unlikely to cause, anything which could, without distortion of language, be
called physical loss or damage. However, in *Tate &
Lyle Industries Ltd v GLC*[7] Lord Templeman[8] said that
in *Junior Books* the pursuer suffered damage to his
property. This suggests that "physical damage" is
being given a wide meaning which includes the deterioration to the product which justifies calling it
defective (as contrasted with deterioration which is
identifiably separate from and can be said to have
been caused by the defect).

Why are courts apparently so unwilling to class-
ify loss as being economic? One answer might be fear
of multiplicity of claims for economic loss. But
this answer is not convincing, because if there is a
problem of multiplicity of claims, it will be the
same regardless of how the loss is classified. Furthermore, *Junior Books* makes it clear that, even if
the loss is perceived as being economic (as it
clearly was in that case), techniques are available
to deal with any problem of multiplicity of claims.
The concern of the House in the *Tate & Lyle* case
seems to have been rather different. To appreciate
the difference it is necessary to draw a distinction
between two juristic bases for liability in tort: a
rights or property basis, and a damage basis. The
classic "property tort" is trespass; the classic
"damage tort" is negligence; nuisance, traditionally
a property tort, is now hybrid.[9] The ground of liability in a property tort is that some right of the

plaintiff has been interfered with. In trespass,
interference with rights is actionable even if the
interference inflicts no loss on the plaintiff; in
property-based nuisance, on the other hand, the
interference is actionable only if damage is suffered
or anticipated as a result of it. The ground of liability in a damage tort is that some act or omission
has caused damage to the plaintiff.[10]

There are a variety of juristic techniques available to deny or limit recovery for infliction of
damage. Perhaps the most straightforward technique
is that adopted by Lord Wilberforce in *Anns v Merton
LBC*, namely to deny recovery if there are reasons
of policy against it. A legally more complex and
opaque technique is that used in *Tate & Lyle*,
namely to acknowledge the existence of damage, but
to assert that the thing (or the right or interest)
damaged is not one protected by the law or
recognized as deserving of protection. The same
technique can be seen at work in *Langbrook
Properties Ltd v Surrey CC*[11] where damage inflicted
by the extraction of percolating waters was held to
be *damnum absque injuria*. Therefore, the assertion
that *Junior Books* suffered damage to their property
was a way of saying that their loss, but not every
negligently inflicted loss, was actionable in
negligence. It is, unfortunately, a very
unilluminating way of saying it which tells us
little about why certain losses are not
compensatable. Another objection to the use of the
property technique is that it introduces a
considerable degree of uncertainty and arbitrariness
into the law. When should a plaintiff be prepared
not only to present argument in terms of the
concepts of the tort of negligence - foreseeability,
causation, remoteness - but also to present
arguments to convince the court that the damage he
suffered was to an interest protected by the law of
torts? What economic interests are protected by the
law of torts? There is no hint in *Junior Books*
itself of property reasoning. In fact, to the
contrary, the contract fallacy, which is a form of
rights reasoning, is specifically rejected by Lord
Roskill.[12] The "damage technique" is not necessarily
any better or worse than the "property technique",
or vice versa, provided adequate reasons are given
for the way and the circumstances in which the
concepts are used. But it is unsatisfactory to
shift without notice from one technique to the
other.[13]

At all events, *Junior Books* strongly suggests
that, in the context of products liability at least,
the "tort" concepts of proximity, knowledge and
reliance will be the preferred juridical categories

for regulating liability for economic loss.

## 2.　Consequential Economic Loss

In the light of all this, what is the current status of the *Spartan Steel*[14] rule that economic loss is recoverable in negligence only if it is consequential on injury or damage to the person or property of the plaintiff? In *Junior Books* Lord Roskill said that *Spartan Steel* would need to be reconsidered in order to decide whether the minority approach of Edmund Davies LJ might not be preferable to that of the majority.[15] Edmund Davies LJ, who dissented in *Spartan Steel*, would have allowed recovery for loss of profits resulting simply from the fact that the factory had to close down for a period, on the ground that such loss was not just a foreseeable result, but also a direct result, of the defendant's negligence. This approach seems to treat the issue of recovery for purely economic loss as one of remoteness of damage. This is an understandable line of reasoning given the facts of *Spartan Steel*, because the plaintiff had suffered some loss which all the judges agreed was recoverable, and so the issue of recovery for purely economic loss could be seen in terms of the extent to which the plaintiff was to be allowed to recover for other (more remote) items of his loss.

However, Edmund Davies LJ's approach is not without difficulties. Once it is conceded that a plaintiff who has suffered damage to property can recover for economic loss which is causally unrelated to that damage, there seems no logical way of denying recovery for economic loss resulting from the defendant's negligence suffered by plaintiffs who suffer no damage to any of their property at all. Their economic loss would not necessarily be any more remote than was *Spartan Steel's*. But proximity between the defendant's negligence and the plaintiff's loss (the remoteness issue) is not the same as proximity between the plaintiff and the defendant (the duty issue). It is this latter proximity which was in issue in *Junior Books*, and it is by no means clear that the approach in that case would enable a plaintiff to recover for interruption to electricity supplies in the absence of some special knowledge on the part of the defendant that an interruption in supply would adversely affect the plaintiff in an unusual way or to an unusual extent. For example in *Birch v Central West County District Council*[16] the defendant electricity authority was held liable for negligent failure to supply the plaintiff, a farmer, with electricity at a sufficiently high voltage to run his cool room, because it knew that he needed the extra voltage, special provision having been made for the supply of high voltage. However, the High Court stressed that there was no general duty owed to electricity consumers generally to supply electricity at a sufficient voltage for normal purposes.

This line of analysis can be carried over into the products liability situation. The sort of economic loss suffered by *Junior Books* - the cost of replacement and expenses associated with replacement - is exactly the same whether suffered by a purchaser of whom the producer has specific knowledge or by an unknown consumer. But there are indications in *Junior Books* that the principles enunciated in that case could not be used to impose a general liability on manufacturers to their consumers; and this was the ratio of the decision of the Court of Appeal in *Muirhead v Industrial Tank Specialties Ltd.*[17] Some of the arguments in favour of this outcome are weak. For example, in *Junior Books* Lord Roskill made the questionable point that consumers ordinarily look to the immediate vendor, and not to the manufacturer, for redress when they acquire sub-standard goods.[18] But regardless of whether the distinction between the known purchaser and the unknown consumer is a sound one, it now seems to be part of the law.

In contrast to Lord Roskill's attitude to *Spartan Steel*, the Privy Council in *Candlewood Navigation Corporation v Mitsui O.S.K. Lines Ltd*[19] held that, as a general principle, a party who merely has a contractual interest in property of another which is damaged by the defendant's tort, is not entitled to recover damages on account of the fact that his contract with that other person has, by reason of the property damage, become more onerous or less profitable. In that case, this general principle was used to deny to a time charterer recovery for hire charges which he was obliged to pay while the ship was being repaired. The Privy Council's ultimate justification for this result seems to have been that <u>some</u> limit has to be placed on liability for economic loss, and that the rule enunciated had the virtues of being supported by a long line of authority and of drawing a definite and readily ascertainable line between liability and no-liability.

The most common objection to the *Spartan Steel* rule is that, although the presence of damage to property does serve in a crude way to limit liability (because damage to property has a lesser propensity to be widespread than does economic loss), its presence or absence is too fortuitous to be legally decisive. The continued validity of this objection

seems to be affirmed by the nature of the Privy
Council's justification for the outcome in the
*Candlewood* case - the Board did not attempt to find a
principled justification for the rule it laid down.
It also seems affirmed by the Board's willingness to
accept the decision in *Caltex Oil (Australia) Pty Ltd
v The Dredge 'Willemstad'*[20] as an exception to the
rule on the basis that, in *Caltex*, there was a high
degree of proximity between the defendant's actions
and the plaintiff's loss. For, although *Caltex* may
be exceptional in the sense that the proximity
approach adopted therein may not produce, in every
case, the opposite result to that which the Privy
Council's rule would produce, it is not exceptional
in the sense that it adds a qualification to the
rule; rather, it endorses a different approach which
was justified in the case itself partly in terms of
the arbitrariness of the "damage to property"
requirement. Finally, the validity of the objection
to *Spartan Steel* seems confirmed by the fact that the
property damage requirement appears to justify a
distinction beween the rights of a time charterer and
those of a demise charterer,[21] even in the absence of
any real difference between the nature of their loss
or the circumstances in which it is suffered.

The fortuity objection to the *Spartan Steel* rule
can be supported by arguing that the presence or
absence of property damage seems irrelevant in cases
where the property damaged is in no way unique or of
peculiar value to its owner. In such cases, damage
to property is simply an economic loss in the sense
that a sum of money equal to the cost of repair or
replacement will fully compensate the plaintiff.
Furthermore, the presence or absence of property
damage is unimportant in terms of insurance.
Insurance is available both against loss of profits
resulting from interruption of power supplies and
against property damage consequential on such
interruption;[22] and whereas, before *Junior Books*,
liability cover was not available in respect of
losses such as those held recoverable in *Junior
Books* or such as that held irrecoverable in *Spartan
Steel*, after that decision insurers were offering
liability cover not only in respect of *Junior
Books*-type loss but also in respect of loss of the
latter type.[23] To what extent cover of this latter
kind will prove, at least in some cases, to be
unnecessary is not yet clear. But the availability
of both loss and liability insurance in respect of
purely economic loss as well as against consequential
economic loss, does suggest that arguments based on
the availability of insurance would not provide a
rationale for making the presence or absence of

property damage crucial.

In fact, however, even for judges who make use of it, loss distribution reasoning based on the availability of insurance plays only a subsidiary part in the analysis of particular cases. This can be seen in Lord Denning's approach in *Lamb v Camden LBC*[24] where he said that houseowners can and should insure against criminal damage to their property and should not seek to recover for it from some other party whose negligent conduct gave the criminals the opportunity to do the damage. On the other hand, his Lordship did not question that the Council should pay for the subsidence caused by their negligence. And yet a typical householder's loss insurance policy would cover such loss. As in *Spartan Steel*,[25] Lord Denning uses insurance arguments just to bolster the results of applying doctrines well established in the law of torts - in *Spartan Steel*, to reinforce the distinction between property damage and purely economic loss, and in *Lamb*, to reinforce an application of rules about remoteness and intervening cause. At all events, there is support for the view that the *Spartan Steel* rule applies only to cases in which A suffers economic loss as a result of damage to the property of B in which he has a contractual interest, and that it does not apply to product liability cases: *Junior Books* was accepted in *Candlewood* but was held to be irrelevant.[26]

The *Spartan Steel* type of case is, of course, factually rather different from a products liability case, most importantly in the respect that in the latter type of case, if there is no physical damage to property of the plaintiff, there is unlikely to be physical damage to anyone else's property either. What, then, is the status of the *Spartan Steel* rule in products liability cases? In the absence of universal first-party property insurance, no-one seems to doubt the desirability of holding manufacturers liable in tort for property damage (plus consequential losses) to any foreseeable sufferer of such damage.[27] It is now also clear that the cost of repairing or replacing defective items in order to forestall personal injury or property damage is recoverable from the manufacturer in tort (on proof of negligence) by the person in occupation or possession of the item when it becomes dangerous.[28] Such a person has the right or obligation to repair or replace, and he can recover whether or not his identity is known to the defendant (so subsequent purchasers can recover). *Junior Books* also supports recovery by such persons for loss of profits suffered while the repairs or replacement are done or,

perhaps, resulting from interruption of production
necessitated by the defectiveness of the product.[29]
One writer has suyggested on insurance grounds that
commercial plaintiffs should not be allowed to
recover for loss of the use of defective products or
premises,[30] but *Junior Books* does not seem to support
this distinction between commercial and private
plaintiffs.

By contrast, it seems that damages for economic
loss arising out of mere defects of quality (both
cost of repair or replacement and consequential
losses) are recoverable in tort, according to the
common law as it has developed so far, only by a
person to whose order and to meet whose requirements
the goods or premises are produced and supplied and
who is, therefore, individually known to the defendant.[31]

Loss distribution arguments might not draw the
same distinctions. For example, if there is an argument for denying to commercial plaintiffs damages for
loss of use, on the ground that they can easily buy
business interruption insurance, it applies as much
to economic loss arising out of defects of quality as
to economic loss arising out of dangerous defects.

It would appear, therefore, that in the products
liability context at least, the *Spartan Steel* rule
has been superseded by later developments. The
distinction between property damage and economic loss
no longer defines the boundary between recovery and
no-recovery. But it does not follow from this that
damages for economic loss will be as freely available
as compensation for property damage, or that every
type of economic loss will be as freely compensated
for as every other type. It does seem, however, that
the logic preferred by the courts for determining the
scope of liability for economic loss in the products
liability context is based on some notion of
proximity rather than on deterrence, loss distribution or insurance arguments.

3.   Distinction between Damage to the Product Itself
     and the Defect

*Anns v Merton LBC*[32] is authority for the proposition
that damages can be recovered in tort for physical
damage to the defective item itself if this damage
causes the product to be a danger to health or
safety. In the 1979 article I argued that the damage
need not be the result of a traumatic incident, but
could be the result just of non-violent deterioration. This proposition is rendered irrefutable by

*Junior Books*, which allows recovery in some cases where the defect and the deterioration are for practical purposes indistinguishable. In the 1979 article I also argued that damages ought to be recoverable for the cost of removing a defect which constituted a potential threat to health or safety, even if it had as yet caused no physical damage or deterioration to the product. *Junior Books* indirectly supports this proposition: it shows that in some cases it may be extremely difficult to draw a distinction between the defect and consequent damage or deterioration, because in that case the floor was really defective only because, and in that, it deteriorated quickly, and the deterioration and the defect could not be dealt with separately - the only way of halting and reversing the deterioration was by replacing the defective floor entirely. In other words, the distinction between the defect and the damage caused by it to the defective product is not crucial. *Junior Books* also establishes a limited exception to the need to show danger to health or safety.

In the 1979 article I suggested that the measure of damages in tort for the fact of defectiveness would always be limited to losses consequential on the defect and would not extend to the fact of defectiveness,[33] this being purely a matter of quality. So, in the case of a dangerous defect, the damages would be the cost of removing the danger, but would not (despite New Zealand authority to the contrary)[34] include any residual depreciation in value remaining after the danger had been removed. Lord Keith (alone) in *Junior Books*[35] adopted a similar line by arguing that the measure of damages was the loss of profits consequential upon the defectiveness of the floor and not the cost of averting or mitigating that loss by replacing the defective floor. However, the distinction between damage consequential on a defect and the fact of defectiveness, while relatively easy to draw where the defect is dangerous, is extremely difficult to draw where the defect is merely one of quality. By definition, if one can recover the cost of bringing a product up to a particular standard of quality or replacing a product with one of that quality, then damages can be awarded for the fact of defectiveness, and there simply will be no residual shortfall in value. So, the proper rule would seem to be that a plaintiff can recover the cost of making the item conform to the relevant standard of quality, or damages for the extent to which it cannot be made so to conform, provided he is in a sufficient relation-ship of proximity with the defendant as defined by

*Junior Books.*[36]   Such a relationship could probably
only exist between a defendant and the initial
purchaser; a subsequent purchaser could recover the
cost of remedying a dangerous defect (provided the
danger arose after he had acquired the property)[37]
but no damages for residual diminution in value of
the property after the repairs had been done.

4.   Liability for Mere Defects of Quality: *Junior
     Books v Veitchi*

(a) Liability Based on Assumption of Responsibility
or Reliance.   Although *Junior Books* can be (and was
to some extent by their Lordships) placed in the
wider context of liability for economic loss, the
issue at stake was really narrower.[38]   There are a
number of ways of viewing exactly what that issue
was.   The first way involves pointing out that the
case did not concern what might be called an accident
between strangers such as occurred in *Spartan Steel v
Martin,*[39] *Weller v FMDRI*[40] or *Caltex v The Dredge
Willemstad.*[41]   Rather, *Junior Books* belongs to a line
of cases, which includes *Donoghue v Stevenson,*[42]
*Hedley Byrne v Heller*[43] and *Ross v Caunters,*[44] in
which there is some sort of bond between the parties.
The bond in *Junior Books* was bilateral, and the
defender had had 'face-to-face' dealings with the
pursuer, as a result of which the defender knew the
pursuer's requirements and the pursuer believed
justifiably that the defender could and would satisfy
those requirements.   But the bond might be unilateral
if, for example, a solicitor is engaged to draft a
will in favour of a named beneficiary who does not
know until after the testator's death that he was an
intended beneficiary.   Bonds which generate liability
in tort may be based on knowledge by the defendant of
the plaintiff and his requirements followed by
conduct, such as the making of statements or the
supplying of goods and services, in such circumstances as betoken a willingness to satisfy those
requirements; or out of expectations reasonably
generated in the mind of the plaintiff by words or
conduct of the defendant that he can and is willing
to provide goods or services to the plaintiff which
meet certain standards of quality.

   Sometimes the mere infliction of damage or loss
is sufficient to generate liability in the tort of
negligence.   But in some cases the infliction of
damage or loss generates liability only because of
some voluntary assumption of responsibility by the
defendant towards the plaintiff;[45] or because, by
engaging in a particular activity or by offering a
particular service, the defendant generates in the

minds of people generally reasonable expectations of
skill or quality of service which would not arise in
the absence of some such additional factor.[46]

The right to expect certain standards of service, or a certain quality of goods, can be bought by
contract; the question in the line of cases presently
under discussion is when a bond other than a
contractual one will entitle a person to enforce a
particular standard or quality.

This way of viewing *Junior Books* stresses the
fact that the sub-contractor had assured the pursuer
that the floor it would lay would meet the latter's
needs. The liability did not rest, as it did in
*Donoghue v Stevenson*,[47] on reasonable expectat-ions
generated merely by the fact of the defendant
engaging in the business of supplying certain products, but on expectations generated by freely given,
but non-contractual, assurances. Manufacturers are
liable for marketing unsafe products simply because
they go into the business of producing and marketing
products. But they are liable for marketing shoddy
products only if, by some additional conduct, they
raise expectations of particular quality standards.
Lord Roskill and Lord Fraser in *Junior Books* thought
that it followed from this that a manufacturer could
not be liable for defects of quality to consumers
generally.[48] But while there may be policy reasons
to deny such liability, there seems no reason in
theory to deny that a manufacturer might, by his
general advertising, generate quite specific
expectations of quality which are not crucially
related to the requirements of any particular
consumer or the particular use to which any consumer
will put the goods. Producers of mass-produced goods
assume certain standard uses and design their products accordingly; and if they lead consumers
generally to expect that the product will be good for
a particular use, there seems no reason to deny that
they have generated reasonable expectations of
quality. Such an argument does not appear to be
inconsistent with *Muirhead v Industrial Tank
Specialties*[49] for, although the Court of Appeal in
that case applied the dicta of Lord Roskill and
Fraser, Robert Goff LJ specifically stated that the
plaintiff had not attempted to argue his case on the
basis of negligent mis-statement.[50]

Under this approach, then, the expectations
raised by the manufacturer's conduct provide a substitute for vertical privity as a ground for recovery. But what about the problem of horizontal privity? Suppose that a third party, not the purchaser

of the product, suffers economic loss as a result of
a defect of quality in the product. If he suffered
personal injury or property damage caused by an unsafe product, he would recover. But could conduct of
a manufacturer ever raise in a non-purchaser sufficiently specific expectations of quality in relation
to goods belonging to another, such as would justify
the imposition of liability? There seems no reason,
in theory, why not; it would all depend on the facts.
The product is the same whoever owns it, and the
third party might have made use of the product
precisely because, as a result of things said or done
by the manufacturer, he thought it was of a
particular quality.

If the obligations of the manufacturer are
measured in terms of the pattern of knowledge, representations, reliance and reasonable expectations
which exist between the manufacturer and the consumer, then the terms of any contractual relationship
between the manufacturer and a middleman should be
irrelevant to determining the rights of the consumer,
unless he can be taken to know of the terms of such a
relationship and to realize that they also govern his
relationship with the manufacturer.[51] Even leaving
aside the provisions of the Unfair Contract Terms Act
1977, the liability of the manufacturer under
*Donoghue v Stevenson* for personal injury could not be
excluded by an exclusion clause in a contract between
the manufacturer and a retailer of which the
consumer was unaware; this is because the liability
of the manufacturer to the consumer rests on the fact
that his product is dangerously defective and that he
put it on the market; it does not rest on or arise
out of the contract between him and the retailer.
His liability is not an extension of his liabilities
in contract to the retailer, but arises independently
in tort out of facts which do not include the contractual dealings between him and the retailer.

Similarly, there seems no reason why liability
for defects of quality, if it arises independently of
any contract between the manufacturer and a middleman, should be excludable by terms of that contract
in the absence of some positive reason why the
consumer should be bound by the terms of that
contract. In *Junior Books* the defender's duty to the
pursuer arose out of the close relationship between
them, not out of the fact that the defender later
contracted with the head contractor to lay the floor
for the plaintiff. If, in their dealings *inter se* no
mention was made of any desire or intention on the
part of the flooring contractor to limit or exclude
his liability for defects of quality, and if ordinary

commercial practice would not lead the purchaser to
expect such exclusion or limitation, why should the
flooring contractor be allowed to exclude or limit
his liability to the plaintiff, unbeknownst to him,
by terms in his contract with the head contractor?
By analogy with certain bailment cases,[52] the
plaintiff could be bound by an exclusion clause if he
must be taken to have consented to the exclusion of
liability, either on the basis of his knowledge or of
ordinary business practice, but not merely by reason
of the existence of the clause.

On the other hand, in *Leigh and Sillivan v
Aliakmon Shipping*, Robert Goff LJ (who was in a
minority in being prepared, in theory, to impose
liability on the shipper) thought that an exclusion
clause in the contract between the seller and the
shipper would bind the plaintiff whether he knew of
its existence or not.[53] The theoretical basis for
this view was the concept of "transferred loss".[54]
One of the implications of this concept is that the
plaintiff's cause of action in tort is, in a sense,
derivative from the breach of duty committed by the
defendant against the party with whom he is in a contractual relationship. Because the plaintiff's cause
of action is derivative, it is limited in the same
way as the cause of action for breach of duty from
which it is derived. By contrast, Oliver LJ considered the cause of action for which the plaintiff
was arguing to be original, not derivative.[55] His
Lordship seems to have concluded from this that if
the plaintiff was to be bound by the limitations and
exclusions contained in the bill of lading, it would
have to be shown that he was aware of them.[56] The
possibility that he might not be aware of them and,
therefore, that he might not be bound by them,
provided for Oliver LJ a reason to refuse to impose
liability to the plaintiff on the shipper. This
difference of opinion brings out very clearly the
true nature of the first interpretation of *Junior
Books* and the centrality to that interpretation of
the concepts of knowledge, expectations and reliance.

(b) <u>Privity of Contract</u>. It is clear from all this
that the first way of viewing *Junior Books* is
inimical to a second, which might be called the
"privity of contract" view. According to this
approach, *Junior Books* can be seen as an attempt, by
using concepts from the law of torts - knowledge and
reliance - to overcome an undesirable consequence of
strict adherence to the doctrine of privity of
contract. The implication of this approach appears
to be that the aim and effect of the development of
the law which *Junior Books* brought about, is simply

to extend the operation of the terms of a contract to a person whom the contractors intended to benefit by the contract, but who is not a party to it and who cannot, therefore, enforce its terms, or sue for bad or non-performance of it. The logic of this approach clearly allows and requires the third party to be bound by terms of the contract which are adverse to him, as well as being able to benefit from terms which are in his favour. The legal basis of liability to the third party is not knowledge on the part of the defendant of the needs and requirements of the third party, or reliance or expectations on the part of the third party, but the fact that the dealings between the defendant and the other contracting party evince an intention to benefit the third party, to contract in such a way as to affect relations not only between themselves but also between the defendant and the plaintiff. So the third party could claim the benefit of such a contract even if, at the time it was made, he did not know of its terms or even of its existence.

As an account of *Donoghue v Stevenson*[57] liability this seems simply wrong. The liability for personal injury or property damage arises out of the facts of dangerous defect and marketing, and not out of any dealings between the manufacturer and the retailer. It could arise even if, for example, the manufacturer gave away a defective product directly to consumers at a trade fair for promotional purposes.

Is the analysis any better for the economic loss cases? Let us look first at a case not concerned with products liability, but which provides an interesting subject for analysis because it is illustrative of the type of case in which the third party might not be aware of the contract between the "producer" and the "middleman" client. The case is *Ross v Cauters*[58] in which an intended beneficiary was deprived of his legacy under a will because the defendant solicitor negligently failed to ensure that the will was properly executed. At first sight, this case might seem easily described as one in which the solicitor and the client entered into a contract, the intention of which was to benefit a third party as well as to provide a contractual service for the testator. But a moment's thought reveals how weak this analysis is. The source of the intended benefit was not the contract, but the will. The testator and the solicitor did not agree together to benefit a third party; rather the solicitor agreed to take care in drawing up a will by means of which the testator would benefit the beneficiary. The document from which the close proximity between the solicitor and the beneficiary arose was the will, not the contract. So, in the case, Megarry VC stressed that the duty of the solicitor to the beneficiary was just to take all due care in drawing up the will, and not the contractual duty owed to his client of doing all he properly could to further the interests of his client.[59]

A case which involved a contract which could quite convincingly be described as one for the benefit of third parties is *Jackson v Horizon Holidays Ltd*[60] (father buys a family holiday). The contract in this case may be an example of a class of contracts (other examples of which would be the ordering of a meal in a restaurant for a party, or the hiring of a taxi for a group) in respect of which the rules of privity need to be relaxed.[61] Here it seems quite clear that the contract is meant to govern relations between the "vendor" and the whole family, party or group.

Does the privity of contract analysis give a good account of *Junior Books*? It seems to fall down in at least two ways. First, as an explanation of what was actually said in *Junior Books*, it shifts the emphasis away from where their Lordships placed it, namely on the closeness of the relationship between the defender and the pursuer, onto the relationship between the defender and the head contractor (of which the court knew nothing). Secondly, the contract between the sub-contractor and the head contractor is unlikely to have been one the intention of which was to confer a benefit on the pursuer. The head contractor was not acting as the pursuer's agent, but as an independent party with interests of its own. The fact that it might have been a term of the contract between the head contractor and the pursuer that the former would employ the defender to lay the floor does not, by itself, mean that, in employing the defender, the head contractor was entering into a contract for and on behalf of, and for the benefit of, the pursuer. So it is implausible to view three-party product liability cases as being "about" privity of contract. It follows that there is no direct relationship between the terms of the contract between the defender and the middleman and the rights of the pursuer.

(c) Contract and Tort. A third way of viewing *Junior Books* is to see it as concerned with the dogma that pure defects of quality are actionable only in contract and not in tort. Apart from the ideological assertion that defects of quality ought only to be

actionable if the plaintiff has bought a warranty of
quality, the main reason for the dogma is that, if
there is no contract, it is difficult to define
exactly what standard of quality the plaintiff can
reasonably expect. We are prepared to fix standards
of safety by external criteria, but when it comes to
standards of quality, we are less willing to jettison
the free market tenet that you get what you pay for.
And yet we are not prepared to allow producers to get
away with just anything, and so we imply certain
warranties of quality into contracts of sale, and
sometimes even make them non-excludable. And, in the
vast majority of cases, the vaguely worded warranties
of merchantability and fitness for purposes are all
that the contract says about quality.

In another field the courts once faced a similar
problem of defining standards of quality, this time
for services. In *MLC v Evatt*[62] the Privy Council
held that liability for negligent mis-statements
would only arise if the maker of the statement was a
professional adviser, or held himself out as willing
to exercise the skill of a professional. One reason
given for this decision was that, unless the standard
of a particular profession could be used as the
criterion for judging the quality of the conduct
which led to the statement, there would be no
objective way of fixing a standard of quality. But
the minority in that case did not accept, nor has the
Court of Appeal in subsequent cases accepted, the
need to provide such an external yardstick. The
courts feel competent to decide whether the defendant
has acted reasonably in all the circumstances,
including the fact that he was or was not paid for
the advice. In particular, the lack of a contract is
not seen as a barrier to the court deciding that the
defendant's service was substandard.

So just how strong is the argument, used in
*Junior Books*, that liability in tort for defects of
quality would have to be exceptional because rarely
will the consumer who is not in a contractual
relationship with the manufacturer have sufficiently
detailed expectations of quality: and, (by implication), because the law will not impose tortious
obligations as to quality in the absence of detailed
expectations?[63] Why should the law of torts not
impose obligations analogous to the contractual
obligations of merchantability and fitness for
purpose? It is no objection that the manufacturer
may not know in detail the purpose for which the
consumer wants the goods, because this is equally
true in contract cases and is taken into account in
defining the defendant's liability - if the use is a

special one, the consumer must make it known to the
supplier if the latter is to be liable for unfitness
for purpose. Besides, all mass-produced products are
made for certain standard, and usually well-known,
purposes. Nor is it any objection that the
manufacturer's liability in tort would have to depend
to some extent on how much the plaintiff paid (you
only get what you pay for), because this is equally
true in contract, and is taken into account in
deciding whether the defendant should be liable or
not. The fact that the manufacturer may not have
determined the price would have to be taken into
account also, but this provides no reason to deny the
possibility of liability in suitable cases. The fact
of the matter is that consumers get at least as many
signals about quality from manufacturers as from
retailers, even when the consumer has no direct
dealings at all with the manufacturer, and it seems
strange that, although these signals flow directly
and not via a middleman, it should be argued that
liability must usually flow through a middleman.

(d) The Nature of the Contractual Chain. A fourth
way of viewing Junior Books involves seeing it as
concerned with the mechanics of business and commercial dealings. There are several aspects of this
approach. One is that, although the pursuer did not
pay the defender for the assurances of quality, he
did pay for them, and the fact that this was via a
head contractor was a matter of irrelevant mechanics.
This line of argument can be taken further. So, it
can be argued that although, in Hedley Byrne,[64] the
particular piece of advice was not paid for by the
plaintiff or by anyone, banks do not give advice for
nothing - 'there is no such thing as a free lunch'.
Somewhere along the line the bank gets something in
return for its advice, and should not be allowed to
rely on an argument that the advice was gratuitous;
the fact that it was voluntarily given by a
businessman raises a presumption that he did not view
the giving of it as a wasted investment. Conversely,
the adviser ought, in appropriate circumstances, to
be allowed to disclaim responsibility for the
accuracy of the answer.[65]

A second string of the argument is made explicit
by Lord Reid in Hedley Byrne.[66] That was a three
party case, but Lord Reid said that the links between
the defendant and the plaintiff were so close that it
could be treated as a two party case. The fact that
the advice was actually physically sought by the
plaintiff's bank was a mere matter of mechanics.
Similarly, it could be argued that the fact that, in
Junior Books, the defender was actually employed by a

head contractor and not by the pursuer, was a mere matter of mechanics, not one of substance. This line of reasoning has relevance in the products liability context in two ways. First, there might be no objection to using the law of tort to repair a breakdown in the contractual chain. For example, in *Lambert v Lewis*[67] the House of Lords was prepared to contemplate the possibility of an action in tort for damages for economic loss by a distributor against a manufacturer, where the distributor had been held liable in contract to a consumer in respect of a defect in the product, but was not able to enforce his contractual right of indemnity against a distributor higher in the contractual chain, because he could not identify the particular distributor from whom he had acquired the defective product. Since tort is here being used, not to evade the contractual chain, but to bolster it up, there is an argument for saying that the tort liability should follow exactly the shape of the liability which would have existed in contract if the chain had not broken.

Secondly, the "mechanics" reasoning is relevant in that, if the contractual chain is mere mechanics, it is arguable that the nature and extent of any liability in tort of one party in the chain to any other should not depend on whether they are in contractual privity with one another. So, if there is an exclusion clause in the contract between the defendant and the head contractor, this ought not to be ignored. Similarly, if there is an exclusion clause in the contract between the plaintiff and the head contractor, the sub-contractor ought to be allowed to take advantage of it. Nor ought the plaintiff normally to be entitled to enforce standards of quality higher than those laid down in that contract.

On the other hand, if the interposition of the head contractor appears not to have been seen by the parties as merely mechanical, then the proper conclusion might be that the provisions of the various contracts were meant to regulate relations only between the parties to them, and were not intended to extend to third parties.[68] It is not clear by what criteria it would be judged whether the contractual set-up was merely mechanical. Why should it not be presumed, for example, that if businessmen set up a chain of contracts, they do so for good commercial reasons, and do not normally intend third parties in the chain to be affected by the terms of the various contracts? Another objection to "telescoping the contractual chain" is that the contract between the defendant and the intermediary might be more favourable to the former than would be (tort) liability based on the "dealings" between him and the plaintiff, thus giving the defendant unilateral[69] power to regulate liability admitted to be bilateral in origin. Similarly, it is not obvious why the rights and obligations of the sub-contractor should be affected by the terms of a contract between the head contractor and the plaintiff, of which he may have no knowledge and over which he has no control. It may be that the use of a chain of contracts ought only to be treated as merely mechanical if all the parties in the chain were involved in the drafting of all of the contracts or, at least, aware of their contents.

And how far is the "mechanics only" reasoning to be taken? Should it matter why the plaintiff has chosen to sue the manufacturer in tort, rather than to sue the middleman in contract? Should the contracts be given a primacy over tort so that remedies in contract would have to be pursued in preference to remedies in tort? Should the plaintiff be allowed to sue in tort to take advantage of more generous rules of remoteness of damage?[70] If the middleman is insolvent, should the purchaser, by suing the manufacturer, be allowed to prevent his damages going into the insolvency and being distributed according to the laws of insolvency, especially given that the sub-contractor is not protected against the effects of the insolvency of the head-contractor? If the plaintiff prefers to sue the manufacturer, because in this way he can avoid souring his relations with the middleman which are more important to him in the long run, should he be allowed to use the law of torts to do this? Or suppose that the plaintiff has settled his claim in contract against the middleman for a sum significantly less than his loss. Should he then be allowed to sue the manufacturer in tort to recover for the balance of his loss?

Again, if the plaintiff is himself in breach of his contract with the head contractor, so that if he sued the latter he would be met by some defence or counterclaim, should he be allowed to avoid having his claim defeated or abated by suing the manufacturer in tort? If the latter can plead against the plaintiff an exclusion clause in his (i.e. the plaintiff's) contract with the middleman, can he also rely on contractual defences the middleman would have had if sued by the plaintiff? And if the head contractor is in breach of his contract with the sub-contractor, should the sub-contractor be allowed to plead this against the plaintiff? Or what if the contract between the head contractor and the sub-contractor is for some reason unenforceable against the former? Will this affect the plaintiff's rights against the sub-contractor? In short, how contractual is the plaintiff's claim?

Another difficult problem raised, but not discussed at any length, in *Junior Books* is that of the subsequent purchaser. Where the product is dangerously defective the position seems reasonably clear - a subsequent purchaser can recover the cost of repair or replacement, provided only that he has title to the premises or product at the time the damage occurs.[71] Where the defect is one of quality, the situation is complicated by the fact that the price is fixed by the previous purchaser, and the purchaser's expectations as to quality may be more dependent on what the vendor says and does than is the case where a first purchaser buys from a dealer or distributor. But, if it could be shown that the price and the purchaser's expectations of quality were significantly affected or influenced by words or conduct of the manufacturer, there seems no reason, in theory, why the fact that the plaintiff is not the first purchaser should necessarily rule out an action in tort.

What about the case of the non-purchaser, the third party who suffers economic loss as a result of a defect of quality? He may well not be able to recover under the "mechanics only" approach because it seems to relate only to persons who are on a contractual chain.

Looking at the situation from the head-contractor's point of view, it might be asked why he should be strictly liable in contract while the sub-contractor's liability in tort is for negligence. If the contracts are mere mechanics should the standard of liability vary according to the cause of action?

These problems are, I would suggest, at least in part the result of seeing the tort action as an extension of, or derivative from, contract. The contract approach attempts, as far as is possible and acceptable, to give effect to the intentions and desires of the parties as expressed in contracts. In some cases, and in *Junior Books* (perhaps partly because so few facts were revealed to the court) the presence of contracts may pose no difficult questions about the proper extent of tort liability as between parties who are on the same contractual chain, but who are not parties to the same contract. But sometimes, the desire to give effect to contractual intentions might clash with tort reasoning which, although concentrating on the relationship between the plaintiff and the defendant, does not primarily seek to give effect to their intentions as revealed and expressed in that relationship, but to construct rights and obligations which seem, as a matter of objective fairness, to express the true dynamics of the relationship. It is by no means easy to discern how the balance between contract and tort ideas will be resolved. There appears to be a desire to restrict *Junior Books* to circumstances where the relationship between the plaintiff and the defendant is very nearly contractual.[72] This limitation removes the need to resolve such of the difficulties discussed above as arise out of the fact that the plaintiff and the defendant have had no dealings *inter se*. But many difficulties still remain, and it may be difficult for the courts to resist adopting solutions based on tort concepts. It has, admittedly, been held in two contexts (that of time charters; and that of passing of risk under a contract of sale), that tort concepts cannot be used to justify recovery for loss suffered in performing a contract as a result of damage to the property of another. But these decisions are of no real use in predicting the course of future development because they were explicitly based on "practical expediency" or "policy" rather than principle.[73]

## 5.  Measure of Damages

What will the measure of damages be for pure defects of quality? The basic measure would, presumably, be the difference between price and value, plus consequential losses not too remote in law. But suppose that, if the goods had been up to standard, they would have been worth more (or less) than what the plaintiff paid for them. Will the plaintiff still recover the difference between price and value, or some greater (or lesser) amount representing the difference between the actual value of the goods and the value of goods of the standard which the plaintiff was entitled to receive? The traditional answer would be that, since *Junior Books* liability is liability in tort and not in <u>contract</u>, then the fact that the plaintiff paid less (or more) than what the goods were worth is irrelevant in assessing his damage. The crucial figure is what he actually paid set against the actual value.

On the other hand, since a main point of requiring a very close relationship between the parties is to provide a basis for measuring the quality which the plaintiff was reasonably entitled to expect, it might be argued that this reasonably expected quality, and not the price paid, should provide the figure to be set against actual value.

The choice between these two measures, it is suggested, should not turn on the characterisation of *Junior Books* liability as essentially tortious or contractual in nature, but on what the basis of the liability is seen as being. If the liability rests on the fact that the defendant has,by his words or conduct, led the plaintiff reasonably to expect goods of a certain quality, then there seems no intrinsic reason why those reasonable expectations should not provide the yardstick for the measurement of damages. It would be to preserve an aspect of the contract fallacy to tie damages in tort for defects of quality directly and inflexibly to the price paid rather than the quality reasonably expected.

## 6.   Limitation of Actions

In *Pirelli v Faber*[74] it was held that where a defect causes damage to a building the cause of action in the tort of negligence in respect of that damage accrues when the damage occurs (or, presumably, when a significant amount of damage occurs, even if it increases later) and not when the damage becomes discoverable. Because the limitation period of property damage is only six years, this is not a satisfactory rule for latent physical damage (the original drafters of limitation legislation seem to have had in mind only cases in which the defendant's negligence and the plaintiff's injury occur more or less simultanously). On the one hand, in practice no action will be brought until the damage is dis- covered, and it may not become discoverable for some time after it occurs. On the other hand, both the date of occurrence and the date of discoverability may be extremely difficult to pinpoint with any degree of accuracy or certainty. The Law Reform Committee has recommended[75] that, in cases of latent damage (which is not defined but means, presumably, damage not discoverable until some time after it occurs), the limitation period should not begin to run until the damage is discovered or becomes reason- ably discoverable. The right to sue would be subject to a long-stop of 15 years after the date of the breach of duty.

What is the position in relation to preventive damages? The economic loss occurs, according to *Anns*, when the need arises to do the repairs in order to remove danger to health or safety. Presumably, by analogy with *Pirelli*, the danger to health or safety arises in the relevant sense when the building or product becomes a danger, and not when the danger becomes discoverable. The danger may reside in the defect itself or in physical damage to which it has given rise or is likely to produce. The mere existence of a defect by itself might not present a danger, and the period would begin to run when it became a danger, even if the danger was not immediately discoverable. If the defect caused physical damage to the building then compensation could be awarded for the cost of repairs, either because the defect had caused physical damage, or on the ground that the physical damage made the building dangerous. In either case the cause of action would accrue when the damage occurred, although in theory the action for physical damage might accrue before the action for preventive damages because *some* damage might occur before the building became dangerous. Presumably, all these rules would be subject to the Law Reform Committee's recommendation that, in cases where the danger is latent, time should not begin to run until it is discovered or reasonably discoverable.

What about liability for defects of quality? When does the *Junior Books* cause of action accrue? Since the loss is economic the "damage" occurs when the substandard goods are purchased. But, under the Law Reform Committee's recommendations, the limitation period would begin to run, in cases of latent defects of quality, only when the defect was discovered or reasonably discoverable.

A further consideration should, however, be noted. Since the plaintiff in a products liability action often has the choice between suing one party in tort and another in contract, there is something to be said for adopting the same rule as to when the limitation period begins to run for both contract and tort actions. The Law Reform Committee's recommendations, however, apply only to tort actions.[76] The Committee specifically rejected the date of breach of duty as the date of accrual, despite the advantage that it would bring tort actions into line with contract actions.[77] So, we can expect more undesirable and pointless litigation[78] in cases of concurrent liability.

7.   Conclusions

(1) There is no important distinction, so far as concerns principles of recovery for economic loss, between defective products and defective premises.

(2)  The distinction between economic loss and physi-

cal damage is not crucial in product liability cases.

(3) The *Spartan Steel* rule probably has no application in product liability cases. Damages for economic loss caused by defective products, but unaccom-
panied by physical damage, can be recovered in
certain circumstances and by certain plaintiffs.

(4) The distinction between the defect and damage
caused by it to the defective product is not crucial.

(5) Damages can be recovered in tort merely for the
fact that a product is defective and worth less than
what was paid for it.

(6) It is not clear how closely the tort liability
for defects of quality recognized in *Junior Books* is
tied to surrounding contracts. One issue is the
extent to which the tortious rights and liabilities
of a party in a contractual chain ought to be defined
with reference to contracts on the chain to which he
is not a party. Another issue is whether parties not
on the contractual chain who suffer consequential
economic loss ought to be able to recover under the
*Junior Books* principles. Much depends on what the
proper interpretation of *Junior Books* is; and on the
solution of a number of difficult technical issues
raised by the decision.

(7) Although the recommendations of the Law Reform
Committee on limitation of actions resolve some of
the problems presented by latent damage, they do not
deal with the difficulty caused, in cases of concurrent liability, by the difference between the rules
as to limitation in contract and tort.

## FOOTNOTES

1     (1979) 95 LQR 117.

2     *Anns v Merton LBC* [1978] AC 728; *Batty v Metro-
      politan Property Realizations Ltd.* [1978] QB 554
      (owners); *Rimmer v Liverpool CC* [1985] QB 1
      (lessors).

3     [1983] 1 AC 520.

4     *Acrecrest Ltd v W S Hattrell & Partners* [1983]
      QB 260; *Pirelli General Cable Works Ltd v Oscar
      Faber & Partners* [1983] 1 AC 1.

5     [1983] 1 AC 520 esp. Lord Keith of Kinkel at p
      535 and Lord Roskill at p 545.

6     Although the pursuers in *Junior Books* did not
      aver that the defective floor as such had caused
      or would cause any consequential economic loss
      (a fact pointed out by both Lord Keith and Lord
      Roskill) they did claim for economic loss conse-
      quential on the <u>need to replace</u> the floor.

7     [1983] 2 AC 509.

8     With whom Lord Roskill agreed 'in all respects
      and for the reasons he gives' (despite his state-
      ment in *Junior Books* [1983] 1 AC 520,545) that
      'in the instant case there is no physical damage
      to the flooring in the sense in which that
      phrase was used in *Dutton*, *Batty* and *Bowen* and
      some of the other cases'. See also *Leigh and
      Sillivan Ltd v Aliakmon Shipping Co. Ltd* [1985]
      QB 350,394-5 *per* Robert Goff LJ.

9     Cane (1982) 2 OJLS 30,54-61.

10    Cf. *Sidaway v Board of Governors of Royal
      Bethlem Hospital* [1984] QB 393,419-20 *per*
      Browne-Wilkinson LJ.

11    [1969] 3 All ER 1424. The rule that economic
      loss is recoverable only if it is the immediate
      causal consequence of damage to the person or
      property of the plaintiff - the *Spartan Steel*
      rule - is analogous. See also *Seale v Perry*
      [1982] VR 192 noted (1983) 99 LQR 346.

12    [1983] 1 AC 520,545.

13    *Tate & Lyle* n.7 supra may be explicable in "dam-
      age terms" on the basis that there was insuffi-
      cient degree of proximity between the parties.

14    [1973] 1 QB 27.

15    [1983] 1 AC 520,547. In *Leigh and Sillivan*
      [1985] QB 350 esp at 379-80, Oliver LJ, in a
      rather confusing judgment, reasserted the
      validity of the *Spartan Steel* rule, and adopted
      it as a partial ground for his decision. Both
      Nourse LJ and O'Connor LJ in *Muirhead v
      Industrial Tank Specialties Ltd* [1985] 3 WLR
      993,1012 felt bound by *Spartan Steel*, but it is
      by no means clear that they adopted the *Spartan
      Steel* rule as the ratio of their decisions.

16    (1969) 119 CLR 652. In *Spartan Steel* Lord
      Denning said that statutory electricity under-
      takers were liable for "direct" physical damage
      but not for economic loss resulting from negli-
      gent interruption of supplies. His Lordship was
      of the view that the same basic rules should
      apply to contractors who negligently interrupt
      the supply of electricity.

17    [1985] 3 WLR 993.

18    [1983] 1 AC 520,547.

19    [1985] 3 WLR 381.

20    (1976) 136 CLR 529.

21    See MacGrath (1985) 5 OJLS 350,365.

22    *Riley on Consequential Loss and Business Inter-
      ruption Insurances and Claims* (6th ed.,
      Cloughton Ed., London, 1985) paras 350-352.

23    This information was supplied by Mr E Hitcham at
      the Colston Symposium on Recovery for Economic
      Loss in Tort held at Bristol University from
      3rd-6th May 1984.

24    [1981] QB 625,637-8.

25    [1973] 1 QB 27.

26    [1985] 3 WLR 381,394.

27    *Muirhead v Industrial Tank Specialties* [1985] 3
      WLR 993; Article 9 of the Council of Europe
      Directive on Liability for Defective Products
      (25th July 1985) defines "damage" for the pur-
      poses of the Directive, to include, with certain
      qualifications, damage to (or destruction of)
      any item of property other than the defective
      product itself. "Defectiveness" is defined in
      terms of unsafeness.

28    *Anns v Merton LBC* [1978] AC 782; *Batty v
      Metropolitan Property Realizations* [1978] QB
      554; *Junior Books* [1983] 1 AC 520,535 *per* Lord
      Keith; 542-4 *per* Lord Roskill. The European
      Directive does not cover such loss.

29    *Junior Books v Veitchi Co. Ltd.* [1983] 1 AC
      520,535A *per* Lord Keith.

30    Smillie (1978) 8 NZULR 109, 121-2.

31    *Muirhead v Industrial Tank Specialties* [1985] 3
      WLR 993.

32    [1978] AC 728.

33    (1979) 95 LQR 117,127-7.

34    *Bowen v Paramount Builders (Hamilton) Ltd* [1977]
      1 NZLR 394.

35    [1983] 1 AC 520,535-6.

36    See further the discussion of *Junior Books* in
      the text which follows.

37    *Anns v Merton LBC* [1978] AC 728; but see
      Robertson (1983) 99 LQR 559; Jones (1984) 100
      LQR 413.

38    As was stressed e.g. by the Privy Council in
      *Candlewood* [1985] 3 WLR 381,394, and by Robert
      Goff LJ in *Muirhead* [1985] 3 WLR 993,1013.

39    [1973] 1 QB 27.

40    [1966] 1 QB 569.

41    (1976) 136 CLR 529.

42    [1932] AC 562.

43    [1964] AC 465.

44    [1980] Ch 297.

45    Cf. *Leigh and Sillivan* [1985] QB 350,394C and
      *Muirhead* [1985] 3 WLR 993,1006G-H, both *per*
      Robert Goff LJ.

46    See *L. Shaddock and Associates Pty Ltd v
      Parramatta CC* (1981) 36 ALR 385; *Sutherland SC v
      Heyman* (1985) 60 ALR 1.

47    [1932] AC 562.

48    See Lord Fraser [1983] 1 AC 520,533D; cf.
      *Lambert v Lewis* [1982] AC 225,264.

49    [1985] 3 WLR 993.

50    *Ibid* at p 1007H.

51    This issue was left undecided by Robert Goff LJ
      in *Muirhead* [1985] 3 WLR 993,1009.

52    Such as *Morris v C W Martin & Sons Ltd* [1966] 1
      QB 716; *Johnson Matthey & Co v Constantine
      Terminal Ltd* [1976] 2 Lloyd's Rep 215.

53    [1985] QB 350,397-8.

54    *Ibid* p 399. The "transferred loss" idea was
      rejected, in a different context, by the Privy
      Council in *Candlewood* [1985] 3 WLR 381,388-9;
      and it seems to have no real application to
      three party product liability cases.

55    [1985] QB 350,382.

56    *Ibid* pp 381-2.

57    [1932] AC 562.

58    [1980] Ch 297.

59    *Ibid* at p 322; but see *Leigh and Sillivan* [1985]
      QB 350,397 *per* Robert Goff LJ.

60    [1975] 1 WLR 1468.

61    See *Woodar Investment Development Ltd v Wimpey
      Construction UK Ltd* [1980] 1 WLR 277.

62    [1971] AC 793.

63    See particularly Lord Fraser [1983] 1 AC 520, 533.

64    [1964] AC 465.

65    Cf. *Leigh and Sillivan* [1985] QB 350,397 *per* Robert Goff LJ.

66    [1964] AC 465 at p 482.

67    [1982] AC 225.

68    Cf. *Candlewood* [1985] 3 WLR 381,389B.

69    Unilateral vis-à-vis the plaintiff.

70    The relevant difference between the tort and the contract rules is that the latter oblige the plaintiff to reveal special circumstances. It could be argued that the plaintiff should not be able to evade this requirement if, in the circumstances of the case, he had the opportunity to reveal, and ought reasonably to have revealed, the special circumstances to the defendant. This approach would generate one rule for cases involving bilateral dealings, and another for cases in which the liability to the plaintiff is based on the raising of expectations by unilateral conduct on the part of the defendant.

71    *Anns v Merton LBC* [1978] AC 728.

72    Liability for negligent mis-statement is, arguably, not limited in this way (see *Candlewood* [1985] 3 WLR 381,393-4). But query whether there is any meaningful distinction between a negligent misrepresentation case, such as *Hedley Byrne*, and a products liability case where the manufacturer makes statements about the safety and quality of his products.

73    See esp Oliver LJ in *Leigh and Sillivan*.

74    [1983] 2 AC 1.

75    24th Report on *Latent Damage* Cmnd 9390, 1984.

76    This is a result of narrow interpretation by the Committee of its terms of reference: Report paras 1.2 and 4.4.

77    Report paras 3.2-3.5. This rule would not yield the same date in both causes of action, but it would reflect the different ground of the plaintiff's claim against different parties in the chain of manufacture and supply.

78    Such as *Midland Bank Trust Co Ltd v Hett, Stubbs & Kemp* [1979] Ch 384.

# THE CIVIL LIABILITY OF MANUFACTURERS IN FRENCH LAW

*Geneviève Viney**

## 1.  Introduction

In France, as in most other industrialised countries, the problem of the civil liability of a manufacturer of goods has preoccupied jurists and the commercial world, especially during the last fifteen years. [1]** Amongst the reasons for this situation a prime factor must be the high number of what we might call "domestic" accidents[2] caused by widely available products like drugs, foodstuffs, cleaning materials, toys, cosmetics and the like. Because of systems of mass-production and -distribution, some of these accidents have had such widespread impact that public opinion has become increasingly sensitive in this area.

At the same time a consumer movement has come into being, whose effect has been not only to increase awareness of the risks to humans and to their enviroment from inadequately controlled industrial activity, but also to cause a number of changes, including changes in the law. Consumer groups have been formed, have actively investigated accidents and in some cases have shown the link between the characteristics of a particular product and an accident that has occurred. These groups have at the same time encouraged and even financially assisted individuals to start legal proceedings; which the latter could not otherwise have undertaken. For this reason, the liability of manufacturers became increasingly asserted. But attempts to use the machinery of the law to achieve this quickly showed how inadequate the existing legal framework was for this purpose.

---

\*    Translation by Philip Britton, University of Warwick (1986) - footnotes omitted.
\*\*   For footnotes see p. 91

Firstly, in relation to procedure it may be re-called that until 1973 consumers' associations had no right to take legal action to protect the inter-ests they claimed to represent. Only with the law of 27 December 1973 (entitled *Loi d'orientation du commerce et de l'artisanat*) did they acquire this right. Article 46 of this law provides that "asso-ciations having as one of their express objects the protection of consumers may, if approved for this purpose, take civil actions before any court related to injury or loss caused directly or in-directly to the interests of consumers".[3] Today, the discussion is about extending this power much further, since the Consumer Law Revision Committee has proposed the introduction of a "collective" or "group" action which would similarly be open to any organisation representing consumers, but which could lead to a judgment directly compensating the injured consumers.

As well as procedural difficulties, it has above all been the substantive rules of law which have proved inappropriate in practice in this area. A manufacturer is under no special legal regulation and therefore falls under the general law, as laid down in the *Code Civil*, on the liability of persons who cause injury or loss to others. This general law provides for two types of liability, one within contractual relations, and the other for extra-con-tractual (delictual) relations, neither really being appropriate to the situation we are considering.

As far as contractual liability is concerned, this normally applies only between the parties to a contract. But the damage caused by a faulty product usually occurs only when it is used by the ultimate consumer who, in the vast majority of cases, has no direct contract with the manufacturer. Further, the obligations stemming from the contract under which the product is delivered (by sale, in particular) look to the fitness of the product for its purpose, rather than directly imposing a duty to ensure its safety.

As for delictual liability, in principle this requires proof of fault against the manufacturer. It is very difficult for someone technically unqualified to establish this and the causal link between fault and the defect in the product.

Taken literally, the rules in the *Code Civil* do not therefore offer the victims of accidents caused by defective products adequate means for asserting the liability of the manufacturer. This quasi-immunity of producers may have been acceptable in the past, but has become ever more intolerable since the possibilities of insuring have made available an effective method of shifting the risk of the cost of liability.

For this reason, at the close of a period in which concern for protection of consumers and the public in general took second place to encouraging maximum production, there has now been a shift in favour of encouraging the quality of production, which requires stricter control of products and increased liability on manufacturers. Especially from the 1960s onwards, the courts realised the need for this shift, and attempted to interpret the *Code Civil* rules in ways more favourable to accident victims and more unfavourable to professionals. In this process they modified - even distorted - the meaning of the statutory rules which they claimed to be applying.

This development has been reflected at government level. A Consumer Law Revision Committee has been created to advise the Secretary of State for Consumer Affairs; it has proposed a series of reforms which would be novel and significant advances in the very area we are considering here.[4]

We can therefore say that, although the economic situation may have slowed its speed, there has been a consistency in the overall movement. On the one hand, case law has, by boldly interpreting the available law, significantly increased the liability of producers for damage caused by their products. On the other, the Government has sought to create a type of liability specific to manufacturers and producers for inadequate safety of their products and for failing to meet the standards reasonably expected by the buying public.

## 2. Increases In Product Liability

This movement has taken the principal form of a diversification in the available legal actions, imposing liability in the most varied circumstances. Additionally, case law and legislature have become increasingly hostile to all clauses limiting liability.

(a) The Legal Actions Available. Among the actions available to impose liability on manufacturers and producers, some are limited to buyers, direct or indirect: these are considered contractual in character. Others are available to third parties: these are delictual in character.

In contract, case law first of all gave a remedy against "hidden defects", under the special rules in articles 1641ff. of the *Code Civil*. But today general contractual liability is equally capable of achieving the same result. Additionally, both principles are now available to the ultimate buyer, including the consumer, as well as to the first.

The "hidden defect" principle probably acquired its prominence because it is based on an objective finding of fact (the defect in the product) which it is then relatively easy to trace back to a failure on the seller's part to fulfil his obligations.[5] This action thus permitted the development of a special set of rules linked to damage caused by things, but based on an earlier personal fault by someone responsible for the object.

The usefulness of the remedy offered by this rule against professional sellers - manufacturers in particular - was significantly extended by case law. Firstly, the notion of "defect" was broadened, so as to class as a material change in the object "anything which makes it inappropriate for its contemplated use", in other words covering effectiveness[6] as well as safety.[7] Next came a bold interpretation of the rules on the extent of liability. Although articles 1645 and 1646 of the *Code Civil* imposed liability on the seller generally only where he knew of the defect which caused damage to the buyer, the courts decided that a professional seller could be presumed to have such knowledge; so in cases of a hidden defect he would be required to compensate the victim. This principle, for which there were historical precedents, was finally established in 1965.[8] Although the principle was framed as a presumption, thus allowing the professional to escape liability by proving that he could not have known of the defect, this escape route was gradually shut off. At present, the *Cour de Cassation* always affirms that the fact of selling by way of trade is sufficient to impose liability for the consequences of hidden defects in the object sold, even if the seller positively proves that he did not know, could not be reasonably expected to know or (even) physically was incapable of discovering the defect.[9] This has in effect become a substantive rule of law,[10] and one which has significantly increased the scope of liability on professionals for product defects.

Under these principles, the manufacturer is in theory no more liable than any other professional

seller. The victim can look to any or all of the
professional sellers who form the distribution chain
to compensate him for the damage caused by a hidden
defect.[11]   But through indemnity actions, it is
usually the manufacturer who ultimately bears the
risk for design or manufacturing defects affecting
the product when it was launched on to the market.[12]

Despite its undeniable effectiveness, this
action has certain limitations, which sometimes prevent victims being compensated. Procedurally,
article 1648 of the *Code Civil* gives only a short
time-limit for action to be begun; the Code does not
lay down an actual limit, but the courts usually
define it as only a few months from the discovery of
the defect.[13]  Furthermore, to succeed in an action,
the plaintiff must prove not only the existence of a
defect in the product, but also the "hidden" or
"secret" quality of this defect in relation to the
buyer[14] and its existence prior to delivery of the
product.[15]   These two conditions cause many legal
actions to fail.

To avoid these hurdles, victims sometimes choose
to base their action on general contractual liability. Is this claim always appropriate? Theoretically, if the courts rigorously applied the words
and spirit of the *Code Civil* in relation to contracts of sale, they would have to hold that acceptance of the product by the buyer is the complete exe-
cution of the seller's duty to deliver, and that no
complaint about the quality can later be enter-
tained, save for hidden defects which, precisely
because of their invisibility, the buyer is presumed
not to have accepted at the moment when he agreed to
delivery.[16]  Case law has however now abandoned this
analysis. Even if a defect comes to light after
delivery, general principles may impose liability on
the seller,[17] which gives victims the chance to cir-
cumvent the conditions of the action based specifically on a hidden defect, in particular the short
time-limit imposed by article 1648 *Code Civil*.[18]
This general liability for products is today widely
defined, as shown by a judgment of the First Civil
Chamber of the *Cour de Cassation* of 22 November
1978, which confirmed that the manufacturer/seller
"has the duty to deliver an effective product appropriate for the user's needs.[19] More recent reported
decisions seem to have softened this duty by holding
that the product must "be appropriate for its
prescribed use".[20]

But it has been in particular the widening of
the duties imposed specifically on manufacturers and

producers,[21] in order to provide better protection
for consumers, that has encouraged the development of
this general contractual remedy. Nowadays, it is
this which is used to combat mistakes or negligent
acts committed by the maker of goods in their design,
manufacture or distribution. The scope of such acts
is very wide indeed.

Firstly, at the design and manufacturer stage,
the courts have accepted that the producer must
"observe standard practice" and that he must show
the diligence reasonably expected by consumers from a
professional of his type.[22] This does not necessarily mean that he must at all times follow all the
relevant standards laid down by AFNOR (Association
Française de Normalisation), for these are legally
binding only when explicitly imposed by ministerial
arrêté.[23] On the other hand, in a concrete case,
failure to follow one of these standards may be
evidence of failure to follow the usual practice,
where the standard enshrines the current state of
knowledge in that area of activity.[24] The existence
of some form of supervision, whether exercised by a
private body or by the State, may similarly be
relevant in showing inadequacy or the precautions
the manufacturer should have taken. Not taking such
external advice into account will usually amount to
fault on the maker's part: coversely, observing all
external rules and gaining all the necessary
approvals does not exclude the possibility of error
and does not confer immunity.[25]

At the distribution stage, the duties on the
manufacturer are also numerous and various.[26] He
must ensure the safekeeping of the product in a form
of packaging which will keep it in good condition and
prevent any injury that it might cause.[27] If he
himself keeps the stocks of the product or does the
work of distribution, then he must prevent the
products deteriorating or becoming dangerous. He
also has a duty of honesty - more often enforced
through criminal law[28] - which prohibits falsifi-
cation, tricks, frauds and incorrect or misleading
publicity.

Before he puts a product on the market, the
maker must in addition check the quality and - above
all - the safety of his product.[29] This duty, first
laid down by case law, has been clearly re-affirmed
by the law of 2 July 1983 on product safety.[30]

By the numbers of cases to which it applies, the
most important of the duties imposed by case law on
manufacturers and producers of products and enforced

by way of general contract law is that requiring
information, advice and warnings against any dangers
that might be created by the product.[31] This duty,
imposed on every professional seller,[32] lies above
all on the producer, who normally has the best possible knowledge of the product, and who is often
required to indemnify intermediate sellers for their
liability to consumers, in particular where the
latter have merely transmitted onwards the notice
drafted by the former and attached to a pre-packaged
product.[33] The duty to give advice does not attach
only to products dangerous in themselves. The duty
covers not only the risks that use of the product
might pose, but also how to use the product. Any
object needing care in use, because of the dangers it
may create, its complexity[34] or the possible impact
of external forces on its ingredients or its
characteristics brings this duty into play. The content of the duty is "to give information so that the
consumer may make use of the product for its
intended purpose without any unpleasant side-
effects".[35] These instructions must be in a clear
and intelligible form, appropriate to the likely
intelligence of the normal users of the product.
Naturally, they must also be accurate and the courts
are even more strict on this requirement, so far as
safety warnings are concerned.[36] Administrative
regulations have in some areas intervened to spell
out and reinforce this duty to provide information,
especially in relation to food products.[37] However,
the *Cour de Cassation* has on occasion suggested that
the duty to inform is in principle not absolute – it
is only a duty to do one's best.[38] But the court has
been particularly strict where the product was a
completely new one[39] and where the consumer was a
layman with no special knowledge. And it applied the
same principle even where the consumer had professional skill, but in an area which would not normally give him the knowledge to realise all the precautions necessary with the product.[40] However, in
the latter case the manufacturer would not be liable
if the missing warning was one of which the
specially qualified buyer could not have been
unaware.[41]

By linking together the general right of action
in contract and the special rules on hidden defects,
case law has therefore sought to ensure the protection of the buyers of products against damage caused
by faulty production or by some other negligence on
the manufacturer's part.

In theory, however, all these contract-based
actions can be exercised only where there are direct

contractual relations between producer and ultimate consumer. In industrial societies, these are rare: there is usually a distribution system which puts intermediate barriers between the two. If, therefore, ordinary contract rules - especially the principle that contracts can legally affect only the parties - had been strictly maintained in this area, then in the vast majority of cases the manufacturers would have escaped legal action, and consumers would be restricted to suing the person with whom they entered into a contract for the product. The manufacturer's liability would have depended on an initial action by the consumer, followed by a series of indemnity actions up the chain. This was what the courts sought to avoid by permitting any buyer of a product to sue any person who is a link in the distribution system, up to and including the manufacturer.[42] This "direct action" (action directe) was created first in relation to the action for hidden defects, where it has existed for a long time.[43] But the availability of the action has recently been widened to general contractual liability;[44] it is thus now universal, giving to the second or later purchaser of a product - in particular the ultimate consumer - the same rights as if he had a direct contract with the manufacturer.[45]

Although most of the side-effects caused by industrial products do affect those that have bought them,[46] they often also impinge on those who have no legal rights at all in the product. When, for example, a defect in a product causes an accident, people or their property who happen to be in the vicinity may suffer the consequences. Such victims can base their claim against the manufacturer only on delictual liability. The courts have frequently accepted that a third party may start an action in delict against a manufacturer, though the plaintiff did not own the product in question.[47]

Such an action in delict is formally based on article 1382 of the Code Civil, which requires the plaintiff to prove negligence on the manufacturer's behalf or that of one of his employees.[48] In fact, findings of negligence are often based on the same grounds as would be used to justify the imposition of contractual liability, had the product's buyer suffered damage and been suing. Hence, inadequate information given on the use or on the dangers of the product will lead equally to the contractual liability of the manufacturer to the buyer and to his delictual liability to third parties.[49] The same can be said for failure to observe any of the rules imposed by legislation or case law on producers so as to protect the safety of individuals and of their

property, for the same facts may be cited by the
courts to impose contractual liability towards the
buyer and delictual liability based on article 1382
of the *Code Civil* towards third parties.[50]

This similarity is especially striking in relation to damage caused by a fault in the product
itself. We have seen how through the "hidden defect"
remedy, a buyer may invoke the contractual liability
of manufacturer or professional seller without having
to prove the negligence of either. The *Cour de
Cassation* has on numerous occasions made it clear
that the fact alone of having put a faulty product
into circulation provides a sufficient basis for the
liability of the manufacturer to a third party, by
reference to article 1382 of the *Code Civil*.[51] The
scope of this principle has recently been clarified
by a judgment which expressly held that it does not
apply to a seller who is not a manufacturer,[52] but
the court implicitly affirmed its rules so far as
manufacturers are concerned.

Some reported cases – more numerous in recent
years – have gone even further. In situations where
a product "has its own internal force capable of
creating a danger" (above all, where it may explode
or catch fire) and where the manufacturer has
retained some control over the product once it has
been delivered, he may be held to have kept custody
(*garde*) of the structure of the product and, as such,
be liable automatically (without need for proof of
fault) for damage to third parties caused by some
internal property of the product, by reference to
article 1384 al. 1 of the *Code Civil*.[53]

The actions available to victims of loss or
injury caused by a product in order to assert the
liability of the manufacturer are thus several in
number and different in character. The effectiveness
of this range of legal actions is further reinforced
by the readiness of case law and statute to attack
contractual terms which tend to limit manufacturers'
liability.

(b) Exemption and Limitation Clauses. In order to
defeat contractual terms limiting manufacturers'
liability, courts use two complementary techniques.

Firstly, they interpret widely the notion of
"gross negligence" (*faute lourde*), holding most
faults of a professional person to have this
character whenever a non-professional or consumer has
suffered loss or injury. Through the maxim "*culpa
lata dol aequiparatur*" (gross negligence is treated

as if intentional wrongdoing), gross negligence has
the same legal effect as intentional fault and as
such allows all clauses exempting from or limiting
liability to be nullified, even where theoretically
valid. The almost automatic reclassification of professional negligence as gross negligence is therefore a highly effective way of eliminating contractual restrictions on the right to recover.[54] But
the validity itself of such clauses has also been
limited, so that at present they are in practice
always prohibited if chosen by professionals at the
expense of consumers.

In the area of delictual liability, there is a
general and traditional bar on all exemption
clauses.[55] The courts have without exception re-
affirmed this principle and have thus had no difficulty in setting aside all would-be contractual
limitations of liability asserted by manufacturers
against the non-buyer victims of products that have
caused injury or loss.

In relation to buyers – immediate and at one or
more removes – liability is based on contract, and
the question must be posed differently, since case-
law accepts in principle that clauses limiting such
liability may be valid.[56] Special principles and
rules have therefore been necessary as the basis for
the courts' refusal to give effect to clauses
limiting the right to compensation.

The starting-point for this development is in
the law on hidden defects. We have seen above how
case law, in order to overturn the *Code Civil* position which originally imposed liability on the
seller of a defective product only if he knew of
those defects, did so by holding the seller to have
such knowledge by virtue of his professional status.
Regarding the professional seller as equivalent to a
seller in bad faith also allowed the courts to strike
out any contractual clause limiting the professional
seller's liability, for article 1150 prohibits all
limitations on the right to recover in case of
intentional wrongdoing.[57]

It is true that the scope of this case law principle has subsequently been challenged; in relation
to situations where both parties are professionals
the *Cour de Cassation* has taken care to preserve the
professional seller's right to limit his liability
towards "a professional in the same field".[58] But,
up to now, this exception has been used only
sparingly[59] – it appears that the maker of a product
is not "in the same field" as the person who merely
distributes the same product.

Be that as it may, hostility to exemption clauses in the relations between professionals and consumers has been uninterrupted. A clear further rule significantly widens this case law principle. Article 2 of the decree of 24 March 1978 giving effect to article 35 of the law of 10 January 1978 (Protection and Information for Consumers), provides as follows: "In a contract of sale entered into by a professional on the one hand and a non-professional or consumer on the other, any clause is null and void as unfair (abusive) which has as its intention or effect the elimination or reduction of the rights of the non-professional or consumer to seek compensation, should the professional fail to discharge any of his obligations". Previously, only clauses limiting liability for hidden defects were prohibited: now, all the obligations of a professional seller have a public policy element attached to them, in relation to the non-professional buyer.

We should add that the Committee on Unfair Terms (Commission des Clauses Abusives), set up by the law of 10 January 1978, has also disapproved of exemption clauses in contracts between professionals and individual consumers and that the Commission almost always recommends their elimination, though not having the power to insist on this.[60]

Products and manufacturers today can therefore no longer count on being able to rely on provisions that they once might have carefully inserted into their "General Conditions of Sale" and distributed to customers, in order to limit liability. Doing so now may even increase their liability. The trend is clear: by developing principles of liability, the courts, more or less effectively backed up by statute, have sought to improve the protection for victims of injury or loss caused by products.

How adequate and comprehensive is the result? We suggest that it is not completely so, and that in a number of directions improvements could still be proposed. Above all, the present system is extremely complex, with the different, overlapping and interlocking contractual and delictual rights of action: we submit that these should be simplified. Most important of all would be to define more clearly the specific duties imposed on the manufacturer, as distinct from the professional seller, of a product. He - or more generally the producer - undertakes a distinct economic activity by putting a new product on the market, and this imposes on him duties towards all those who may use the product or who may be affected - especially in relation to safety - by its use. Linking these duties to the contract of sale is clearly artificial, for the producer's duties are in reality owed to the public at large.

It is therefore not surprising that energy has been directed towards the creation of a special type of liability, imposed on producers as such and largely divorced from the traditional distinction between contractul and non-contractual liability.

3.  Towards the Creation of Producer and Manufacturer Liability

The arguments for abandoning a contractual framework for producers' liability seem most self-evident in the areas of product safety, in which the whole community has an interest and which cannot be regarded as the concern only of contracting parties. We shall see that the notion of liability on the producer, based on a finding of want of safety by reference to the public's legitimate expectations, has already been implemented, although the contours of this new principle are not yet clear. On the other hand, in order to define failure on the producer's part and to sanction his inattention, it is still usual to refer to contractual notions. For this reason the proposed system of liability based on the producer's putting a product on the market does not meet the needs of the average consumer, and is therefore not yet, we submit, ready for implementation.

(a)  Liability for Unsafe Products. Many countries have since 1970 felt the need for a special system of producer's liability for unsafe industrial products. At the time, this movement gave rise to two draft international conventions, intended to unify the law. The first, drafted under the Council of Europe, was opened for signature by Member States on 1 January 1977: this is the European Convention on Products Liability in Regard to Personal Injury and Death which France has signed but which has not yet received enough ratifications to enter into force. The second is the text which, after several drafts, on 25 July 1985 became the European Communities Council Directive "on the approximation of the laws, regulations and administrative provisions of the Member States concerning liability for defective products".

In France, the question was raised again in 1982 by the Consumer Law Revision Committee, which drafted various Bills intended to protect consumer safety. One of these has now been passed by Parliament: the law of 21 July 1983, some of whose provisions

significantly affect the liability of producers of
unsafe products. A second Bill, still at the drafting stage, proposes a new special system of liability of a producer for his products.

The aim of the law of 21 July 1983 was to organ-
ise the prevention of accidents caused by industrial
products. It does not therefore directly affect producers' liability, but some of its provisions may
nevertheless affect the determination of questions
of liability.[61] This is especially true of article
1 of the legislation: "Products and services must,
when used normally and under conditions reasonably
foreseeable by a professional, be as safe as may
legitimately be expected and not injure anyone".

In this formulation, the article is an attempt
to give legislative expression to the most important
developments in case law on producers' liability.
The reference to "as safe as may legitimately be
expected" represents a choice of an objective standard of safety, exactly in line with the harmonisation (noted above) between the protection the
courts offer under contract law to the buyer and
that available under the law of delict to third
parties.

We should add that the right to safety subsists
not only for use of the product under normal conditions, but also under abnormal conditions, where
these would have been reasonably foreseeable by a
professional, suggesting that only a high degree of
contributory negligence on the victim's part will
leave the producer free of liability. This therefore
confirms and reinforces earlier developments,
increasing the obligations on producers concerning
the safety of products.

But the contribution of the law of 21 July 1983
is not limited to this statement of principle.
Several of its other provisions contain important
innovations in this area.

Firstly we must mention that for the first time
a generally applicable rule has enshrined the notion
of "liability for first putting on the market"
(*responsabilité de première mise sur le marché*). To
this end article 11-34 adds the following words to
the law of 1905 on fraudulent practices:

"At the moment of first being put on the market,
all products must conform to the rules in force
on public safety and health, on fair trade
practices and on the protection of consumers.

The person who first puts a product on the market thus has a duty to check that the product does so conform. At the request of the officials responsible for enforcement of the present law, he shall give evidence of the checks and enquiries that he has undertaken."

This rule thus focuses on the producer (manufacturer or importer) liability which might arise from failure to observe rules relating to the launch of a product. These rules are nowadays numerous and demanding. Certain classes of product which are especially dangerous for man or the environment — pharmaceuticals, poisons, agricultural pesticides — cannot be marketed without prior approval, this being conditional on the results of tests and enquiries which are laid down in minute detail. Other types of product, like chemicals[62] and cosmetics, cannot be marketed without details being first formally deposited with a branch of the Administration. Even for products not subject to these special procedures of prior authorisation or declaration, the law of 10 January 1978 (as extended by the law of 21 July 1983) gives the administration very wide powers of intervention and control. The Administration may give appropriate organisations the power to control certain products and may lay down specific rules concerning the manufacture, distribution, labelling, storage and conditions of use of a product and the conditions of hygiene and security to be observed by anyone taking part in any of these processes. It may also order the giving of public warnings or instructions or precautions that should be taken. As the person responsible for the launch of a product onto the market, a producer must therefore be sure that all these requirements have been fulfilled and he will ultimately be liable to any victims if he fails to do so, for the plaintiffs will be able to show the causal link between this breach and the injury or loss they suffered.

Finally, it should be added that the law of 21 July 1983 gives power to administrative authorities to order the temporary stopping of distribution of a product, the halting of its production, its outright withdrawal from the market, its recall with a view to modification, refunding of the purchase price, replacement or even ultimately its destruction: these powers leave manufacturers open to actions by wholesalers, retailers and even consumers, who are thus temporarily or permanently deprived of the product they have bought.

It is therefore clear that the law of 21 July 1983 has made an important contribution to the creation of a special system of responsibility for product safety which rests on manufacturers and producers.[63] This change will not, however, be complete until a law directly addressing the liability of manufacturers has been passed.

The Consumer Law Revision Committee, realising this, itself drafted a Bill, linked to the Bill on which the law on 21 July 1983 was based. The central aim of the drafters of this Bill[64] was to introduce for France a system largely derived from the principles in the Strasbourg Convention and from what was then the draft of the Brussels Directive. Like these two, the draft does away completely with the distinction between contractual and delictual liability, the victim's protection not varying, whether or not he had a contract with the defendant.

As for the scope of the proposed new principle, it would be available to any person injured by any product (movable or immovable) which has been put on the market, but it only covers compensation for physical injury. Here it differs from the European Directive, which covers only movables but which extends to some damage to property (where used personally by the consumer).

Liability would be based on "putting onto the market a product which is less safe than might legitimately be expected": it is not a question of fault or even of a "defect" but a finding of objective fact, the shortcomings of the product by reference to the legitimate expectations of the public. Like the European rules, the Bill does not impose liability on any seller, but on the "producer", who will usually be the manufacturer. Only when this person is out of the victim's reach can someone else be sued in the producer's place.[65]

The proof which the victim would have to give would not be hard, since he would only have to show that he had suffered injury caused by the product. He would not even have to show that at the moment of putting the product on the market, it was less safe than could legitimately be expected. This, it should be noted, is a major difference from liability based on hidden defects, where the victim has to show that the defect was not apparent on delivery; we need hardly stress how severe the proposed rule is on the manufacturer.

The first draft does, however, make certain defences available to the latter. Firstly, he can escape liability by showing that it was not he who put on the market the product which has caused the injury. And he may prove that the product was not defective when first put on the market - that is, that its design and manufacture made it as safe as might legitimately be expected. Although evidence to this effect may be hard to collect, if the manufacturer can do so he will not be liable. Similarly he can protect himself by proving *force majeure* - that is, even external to him which he could neither foresee nor prevent and which caused the injury complained of. This external event may be some inevitable accident (*cas fortuit*), the act of a third party or the act of the victim.

As far as inevitable accident and the act of a third party are concerned, these do not limit the rights of the victim against the manufacturer, unless they have the necessary characteristics of "unforeseeability" and "irresistibility"; and he does not lose his normal right to sue for a contribution or indemnity anyone who has been responsible with him for the injury. On the other hand, the victim's use of the product "under abnormal conditions" may be argued by the defendant in order to reduce his liability, on condition that he could not have foreseen this abnormal use.

Knowledge by the manufacturer is clearly not a pre-condition for his liability, which continues even if he proves that he could not have known, and the draft makes clear that "development risks" - unknown by anyone at the moment the product was launched - do lie on the producer. (This is a further contrast with the European Directive.)

In relation to the scope of liability, the Committee has opted for full compensation with no ceilings. And in order to guarantee that victims will receive their awards, it has provided for the creation of central funds for specific sectors of the economy (*fonds de garantie*), which will compensate for physical injuries caused by products or services, where the person normally liable, or his insurer, is totally or partially insolvent.[66]

We should add that the draft lays down two time limits which restrict the producer's liability. Ten years after the first launch of a product this liability will expire, and the victim will have three years to commence proceedings from the date on which he knew that the injuries resulted from the defective product and knew the producer's identity.

Finally, this system of liability being imposed by statute, clauses limiting or excluding liability will be prohibited. However, in a way which is hard to reconcile with its obligatory character, the drafters of this Bill have decided that the new system will not replace the existing rules; victims will therefore have a choice between the new rules and the present system.

Any real chances this draft may have had of being passed by Parliament have been fundamentally changed by the Council of Ministers' adoption of the Directive of 25 July 1985. The French legislature is now bound, within three years, to change French law in such a way as to fit with the Directive. Since the Reform Committee's concerns overlap with those expressed in the Directive, it is likely that those responsible for bringing French law into line with the European rule will start with a careful examination of the Committee's Bill. However, where the Committee's proposals diverge from those adopted in the Directive, the latter will now have to prevail.

But is this consumer law reform movement limited to liability based on the unsafe character of products? Does it also extend to liability for products whose quality is inadequate?

(b) <u>Liability for Defects in Quality</u>. At first sight, it seems reasonable that the manufacturer's special role in the design, making and launch of the product should give rise to a special liability for a product which fails to meet the legitimate expectations of the consumer. In this case, as with safety, treating the manufacturer in the same way as a professional seller seems neither logical nor completely satisfactory.

Most commentators at the present time believe that applying contract remedies derived from the law of sale is sufficient to protect the victim of this sort of damage, the manufacturer being able to be sued as original seller, either by the victim through the "direct action" which passes to each ultimate buyer or by indemnity action, if intermediate sellers can successfully prove that the defect antedated or accompanied the product's launch on the market. The Consumer Law Reform Committee broadly accepted this analysis in its Bill on product quality:[67] this imposes the same liability on all professionals who, as part of a contract transaction, supply an object - movable or immovable - which "fails to meet the legitimate expectations of the consumer".

Does this mean that the Commission plans no changes in the law on the producer's liability for products which are not up to standard? Not so.

Firstly, we must stress that the present distinction between an action for hidden defects and a general right of action in contract would disappear, and be replaced by a single general action available in all cases of "sub-standard" goods or services.

Additionally, the question of standard would be tested not only by reference to the contract terms but by reference to a more objective notion of "the legitimate expectations of the consumer".[68] The change would be comparable to that which has occurred in relation to safety.[69]

At the same time one finds, as in the case of safety, an obligation to check or verify which is especially applicable to the person responsible for first putting the product onto the market. In effect the text requires that, 'every person who puts goods or services onto the market in the course of a business must first insure that they meet the legitimate expectations of consumers'. Here we can see the germ of a special liability imposed on manufacturers and producers. This liability could become of great importance since a further clause[70] provides that "Administrative regulations may define in what circumstances goods and services are in accordance with the legitimate expectations of the consumer" and to this effect gives very extensive powers to administrative authorities to regulate methods of production and to decide what checks manufacturers ought to make. Moreover, the Bill lists a whole series of sanctions following from a finding that a product is "sub-standard". It gives a judge the power to order a product to be "made to meet the legitimate expectations of consumers", "withdrawn from the market" or the public to be informed by way of a "message" of the failure of the product to come up to standard.

We may add finally that this Bill explicitly reaffirms the "direct action" the consumer enjoys against the manufacturer and successive sellers and that it extends its scope "to a succession of contracts for services as well as to a succession of contracts of sale and for services".

To conclude, although the reforms proposed for failure of products to come up to standard are less far reaching than those for unsafe products, they nevertheless are evidence of a new awareness of the special position of manufacturers and producers in comparison with simple sellers. Generally speaking, it seems very likely that the next few years will see the introduction in France, as in most other industrial nations, of a new system of liability, specific to manufacturers and producers, separate from the rules on contracts of sale and derived from a wish to satisfy the legitimate demands of the public.

## FOOTNOTES

1    Voir à ce sujet, parmi de très nombreux ouvrages et articles, J F Overstare : La responsabilité du fabricant de produits dangereux, Rev.trim. dr.civ. 1972, p. 485 et s.: P Malinvaud La responsabilité civile du fabricant en droit français, Gaz.Pal. 1973.I.Doc. p. 463 et s.: J Bigot, La responsabilité contractuelle pour vice du produit livré; et La responsabilité extracontractuelle pour le produit livré, Jurisclasseur Responsabilité civile, Fasc. XIXter, 3e et 4e cahiers; La responsabilité des fabricants et distributeurs, colloque 30 et 31 janvier 1975, Université de Paris I, Economica 1975; J Ghestin : Conformité et garanties dans la vente, L.G.D.J. 1983; Rapports de MM Sainte Affrique et Mariott au Xe Colloque juridique international de Lisbonne, 7-10 octobre 1983, Rev.gen.ass.terr. 1983, p. 574 et s.; J Revel 'La Responsabilité civile du fabricant', Thèse, Paris 1975.

2    Voir l'enquête réalisée par la Fédération nationale des coopératives de consommateurs en 1981 (Resultats évoqués dans le rapport de R Jager au Sénat sur le projet de loi relatif à la sécurité des consommateurs, J.O. Doc. Sénat 2e session 1982-1983, No. 345, p. 8 et 9).

3    Cette possibilité a été largement utilisée par les juges du fond. Mais la Cour de Cassation lui a apporté une restriction importante - et peu justifiée à nos yeux - en décidant le 16 janvier 1985 qu'elle ne peut s'appliquer qu'en cas d'infraction pénalement incriminée et non sur le fondement d'une simple inexecution contractuelle (D. 1985 p. 317).

4    Voir J Calais Auloy : Propositions pour un nouveau droit de la consommation, La Documentation française, 1985. Ces réformes sont sous les verrous, tout à fait dans la ligne des

textes européens, notamment dans la Directive du Conseil des Communautés européenes du 25 juillet 1985 relative au rapprochement des dispositions législatives, réglementaires et administratives des Etats membres en matière de responsabilité du fait de produits defecteux.

5   Voir J Ghestin, Conformité et garanties n.1, .... No. 8 à 31.

6   Voir B de Sainte Affrique, rapport précité, n.1, Rev.Gen.ass.terr. 1983, p. 576 et s.; J Ghestin, Conformité et garanties n.1, ..... No. 208 à 218; voir Com. 29 mai 1984 J.C.P. Actualités 4 juillet 1984, Civ.[2] 26 mars 1985, Bull.Civ. No. 79 p. 51; Civ.[3] 18 avril 1984 J.C.P.1984.IV p. 198; et pour un cas de pure et simple non-conformité, Poitiers, 4 aout 1983 J.C.P. 1984.IV, 195.

7   V. Civ.[1] 28 novembre 1979 D.1985 p. 485 1ère espèce, note J Huet.

8   Civ.[2] 14 janvier 1965 D.1965 p. 389.

9   Com. 27 novembre 1972 Bull.Civ. IV N.266 p. 282; Civ.[3] 17 juillet 1972, Bull.Civ. III No. 473 p. 344; Comm. 15 novembre 1971, D.1972 p. 211; Civ.[1] 12 mars 1980 Bull.Civ. I No. 84 p. 69.

10  Voir J Ghestin, Conformité et garanties n. 1, ... No. 258.

11  J Ghestin, op.cit. n. 1, No. 259.

12  Voir Com. 15 novembre 1983 J.C.P. 1984.IV p. 31, Bull.Civ. IV No. 311 p. 269; Com. 15 janvier 1985 Bull.Civ. IV No. 25 (vice indécelable). Toutefois, le fabricant n'a pas à garantir le revendeur qui a lui-meme vendu un produit dont il connaissait le défaut, Civ.[1] 13 juillet 1985 J.C.P. 1985.IV p. 32.

13  J Ghestin, op.cit. n. 1, No. 23 et s. - Voir sur la fixation du point de départ de ce delai, Com. 20 mars 1984 J.C.P. 1984.IV p. 172.

14  Voir Com. 24 janvier 1984 J.C.P. 1984.IV p. 107.

15  J Ghestin, op.cit. n. 1, No. 9 à 22. Voir notamment Com 18 janvier 1984 J.C.P. 1984.IV p. 97; voir également Civ.[1] 16 novembre 1984 D.1985, p. 485 2e espèce, note Huet.

16  J Ghestin, op.cit., n. 1, No. 223 et 224.

17  J Ghestin, op.cit. n. 1, No. 225: G Viney, *La responsabilitié* Vol. 1 : Conditions (1982) No. 765.

18  Voir Civ.[3] ler février 1984 J.C.P. 1984.IV

p. 115; Civ.[1] 9 mars 1983 Bull.Civ. 1983.I No. 92 p. 81, J.C.P. 1984.II 20295 note P Courbe. Ass. plenière 7 janvier 1986 D.1986 Flash 27 février.

19  J.C.P. 1979.II.19139.

20  Com. 15 janvier 1980 J.C.P. 1980.IV p. 125; Civ.[3] 21 octobre 1981 J.C.P. 1982.IV p. 16. Voir également, pour une vente de matériel informatique, Paris, 4 novembre 1983 D.1984. I.R. p. 160; Com. 15 juin 1983 D.1984. I.R. p. 175.

21  Ces obligations sont parfois présentées comme des "accessoires de l'obligation de délivrance" (voir, pour l'obligation d'information et de mise en garde, Civ.[1] 27 février 1985 Bull.civ. I No. 82 p. 75), mais parfois elles sont rattachées à l'article 1135 du code civil (voir également pour l'obligation d'information et de mise en garde, Civ.[1] 3 juillet 1985 J.C.P.1985.IV p. 320).

22  Voir J Bigot, op.cit.n. 1, Jurisclasseur Responsabilité civile, fasc. XIXter, 4e cahier, No. 61, 62, 68 à 70; G Viney, in La responsabilité des fabricants et distributeurs, précité n. 1, No. 12, p. 78.

23  Art. 12 décret 26 janvier 1984.

24  Voir G Viney, La responsabilité : conditions, n. 17 No. 461.

25  Voir J F Overstare, article précité n. 1, Rev.trim. dr.civ. 1972, p. 485, No. 61 à 65. Voir, en matière pharmaceutique, l'arrêt particulièrement explicité et intéressant de la Cour de Paris, 15 decémbre 1983 (Rev.trim.dr.sanit. et soc. 1984, p. 202, D.1985 p. 228 note J Penneau.

26  Voir G Viney, in 'La responsabilité des fabricants et distributeurs"n. 1, p. 79 No. 13.

27.  Com. 6 mai 1975 *SA le matériel téléphonique (LMT)* contre *La Concorde et la Sarl Droguerie Quincaillerie Gaume et fils* et, en matière de vente de gaz, TGI Libourne 2 février 1978 G.P. 1978.I. som. p. 210; Civ.[1] 23 octobre 1984 Bull.Civ. I No. 275 p. 234 (Le fournisseur du gaz commet une faute s'il procure du gaz à pression élevée dans des conditions dangereuses eu égard à la structure et l'emplacement des canalisations).

28  Voir B Bouloc, "La responsabilité pénale des fabricants et distributeurs de produits" in "La

responsabilité des fabricants et distributeurs",
n. 1, p. 339 et se.; J C Vindreau : La respon-
sabilite pénale du fabricant de produit, thèse
(dactyl.) Paris I, 1984.

29     Voir Civ.[1] 8 janvier 1985 Bull.Civ. I No. 11
p. 10.

30     Article 11-4 ajouté à la loi du 1er août 1905
par la loi du 21 juillet 1983.

31     Voir notamment J F Overstare article précité, n.
1, Rev.trim.dr.civ. 1972 p. 485, No. 14 à 23;
P Malinvaud, article précité n. 1, Gaz.Pal.
1973.2. Doc. p. 483; D Nguyen Thann : Techniques juridiques de protection des consommateurs, thèse 1969, No. 781 et s.; J Bigot,
Jurisclasseur Responsabilité civile, Fasc.
XIXter, 4e cahier, No. 82 à 94; D Nguyen Thann
et J Revel : La responsabilité du fabricant en
cas de violation de l'obligation de renseigner
les consommateurs sur les dangers de la chose
vendue, J.C.P. 1975.I.2679; J Revel, thèse précitée n. 1, p. 197 et s.; J Calais Auloy, Droit
de la consommation, Précis Dalloz No. 68; F
Chabas, Informer les utilisateurs, Revue de
CNPF, 1975, p. 41 et s.; G Viney : La responsabilité : conditions n. 12, No. 511; J Ghestin,
Conformité et garanties, No. 98, 269 et s., 321.

32     Voir Civ.[1] 23 avril 1985 Bull.Civ. I No. 125
p. 115; Civ.[1] 27 février 1985 Bull.Civ. I No.
82 p. 75 a qualifié cette obligation "d'acces-
soire de l'oibligation de delivrance". Mais
Civ.[1] 3 juillet 1985 l'a rattachée à l'article
1135 du Code civil.

33     Voir Civ.[1] 14 décembre 1982 Bull.Civ. I No. 361
p. 309; Civ.[3] 10 mars 1982 Rev.droit immob. 1982
p. 519. En revanche, dans ses rapports avec
l'acheteur non initié, le vendeur non fabricant
ne peut se prévaloir du fait qu'il a reçu
lui-même une information insuffisante du
fabricant : voir Civ.[1] 27 février 1985 Bull.Civ.
I No. 82 p. 75.

34     Voir, pour un matériel informatique, Paris 27
mars 1984 D.1985 I.R. p. 42 observ. J H.

35     Voir J Revel[1] thèse précitée n.1, p.208 et, par
exemple Civ.[1] 23 avril 1985 Bull.Civ. I No. 125
p. 115; Civ.[1] 3 juillet 1985 J.C.P.1985.IV
p. 320.

36     Voir, par exemple Civ.[1] 14 décembre 1982 Bull.
Civ. I No. 362, observ[1] G Durry, Rev.trim. dr.
civ. 1983 p. 545; Civ.[1] 11 octobre 1983 Bull.
Civ. I No. 228 p. 204, D.1984 p.234 note
F Chabas; Paris 24 mars 1982 D.1982.I.R. p. 188
note E Wagner.

37    Voir notamment le décret du 12 octobre 1972  sur
      l'étiquetage des produits alimentaires.

38    Voir  Civ.[1] 23 avril 1985 Bull.Civ. I  No.  125
      p. 115.

39    Civ.[1] 7  novembre 1984  Rev.droit  immob.  1985
      p. 159.

40    Civ.[1] 23 avril 1985 B.C. I No. 125 p. 115; Civ.[3]
      17 octobre 1984 J.C.P. 1984.IV p. 355.

41    Com. 5 février 1985 B.C. III No. 48 p. 41.

42    Voir  notamment  P Le  Tourneau,  Conformité  et
      garantie dans   la   vente  d'objets  mobiliers
      corporels, Rev.trim.dr.com. 1980 p. 231 et  s.,
      No. 92 et s.; J Ghestin, Conformité et garanties
      n.  1,  ..., No. 324 et s.; H L J Mazeaud  et  F
      Chabas, Traité t.III, ler vol. 6e ed. No.  2190;
      G Viney, La  responsabilité : conditions,n.  12,
      No.  750;   P Malinvaud,   L'action  directe  du
      maître  de  l'ouvrage contre les  fabricants  et
      fournisseurs de matériaux composants D.1984  Ch.
      p.41  et s. et p.47 et s.; Rev.droit  immobilier
      1984  p. 1 et s.; M Espagnon, Remarques  sur  le
      concours  des actions nées du vice caché  ou  de
      la non-conformité du navire en cas  d'acquéreurs
      successifs  ou d'utilisateurs successifs,  Revue
      "Le droit maritime français", février 1984  p.67
      et s., notamment p.70 à 74, et 78 à 81.

43    Voir  notamment Com. 27 avril 1971 J.C.P.  1972.
      II.17280 lère  espèce, note Boitard  et  Rabut,
      Com.  15 mai 1972 Bull.Civ. IV p. 143 No.  144;
      Com.  16  octobre 1973 Bull.Civ. IV p.  256  No.
      285;  Civ.[3] 5 avril 1978 J.C.P. 1978.IV p.  189;
      Com. 18 octobre 1982 J.C.P. 1983.IV p. 14; Com.
      17  mai 1982 Bull.Civ. IV No.  182,  Rev.trim.
      dr.civ.  1983, p. 135. La cour de  cassation  a
      longtemps  fait exception à cette  jurisprudence
      dans  les rapports entre maître de l'ouvrage  et
      fabricant  d'un  matériau  incorporé  dans  son
      immeuble. (Succession d'un contrat de vente  et
      d'un  contrat  d'entreprise).   Mais  la  lère
      chambre civile a décidé le 29 mai 1984  d'étendre
      a  ce cas la solution admise pour  les  ventes
      mobilières (Bull.Civ. I  No.  175  p.  149).
      Cependant  la 3ème Chambre civile n'a pas  suivi
      cette  jurisprudence et elle a  réaffirmé  que,
      dans  cette  hypothèse,  la  responsabilité  du
      fabricant  est délictuelle (voir Civ.[3] 19  juin
      1984 J.C.P.1984.IV p. 280; Bull.Civ. III No. 120
      p.  95;  Civ.[3] 17 octobre 1984  J.C.P.  1984.IV.
      p. 355.  Les arrêts Civ.[1] 29 mai 1984 et  Civ.[3]
      19  juin 1984 ont été commentés par A  Benabent,
      D.1985 p. 213 et par P Malinvaud J.C.P.  1985.

II.20385; voir également les observations de P Remy, Rev.trim.dr.civ. 1985 p. 406; P Malinvaud et B Boubli, Rev.dr. immob. 1984 p. 420). L'Assemblée plénière a donc du intervenir. Elle a consacré, le 7 février 1986, la jurisprudence de la 1ère Chambre civile (arrêt encore inédit) D.1986 Flash 27 février, 1986.

44  Civ.[1] 9 mars 1983 Bull.Civ. I No. 92, p. 81.

45  En revanche, par application de la règle du "non cumul des responsabilités contractuelle et délictuelle", elle lui retire le[1] bénéfice de l'action délictuelle. Voir Civ[1] 3 mai 1984 Bull.Civ. I No. 149 p. 126; Civ.[1] 13 novembre 1986 Bull.Civ. I No. 303 p. 258.

46  Ou, par contrecoup, ceux le leurs assureurs qui, étant subrogés, doivent également agir sur le terrain contractuel : voir Civ.[1] 3 mai 1984 J.C.P. 1984.IV p. 322.

47  G Viney, rapport précité in "La responsabilité des fabricants et distributeurs", n.1, No.6 p.71.

48  G Viney, Ibidem, No. 10, p. 76.

49  Voir Civ.[1] 11 octobre 1983 Bull.Civ. I No. 228 p. 204 qui a admis la responsabilité du fabricant pour manquement à l'obligation d'information en qualifiant cette responsabilité de "contractuelle" à l'égard de l'acquéreur et de "delictuelle" à l'égard des victimes non propriétaires (brulees dans un incendie provoque par l'utilisation du produit). Voir également Civ.[3] 17 octobre 1984 J.C.P. 1984.IV p. 355. Ajoutons qu'entre professionnels qui participent à des activités connexes, le manquement au devoir d'information réciproque est quasi délictuel : voir Civ.[3] 3 octobre 1984 J.C.P. 1984.IV, p. 338.

50  Voir Civ.[1] 20 janvier 1979 Bull.Civ. No. 69 p. 54.

51  Voir Civ.[1] 21 mars 1962 Bull.Civ. 1962.I.155, Civ.[1] 5 mai 1964 Bull.Civ. 1964.I.181; Civ.[2] 16 mars 1966 Bull.Civ. 1966.II.249; Civ.[3] 28 avril 1972 Bull.Civ. III No. 233 p. 167; Civ.[1] 18 juillet 1972, Bull.Civ. I No. 189 p. 164; Civ.3 5 décembre 1972 D.1973 p. 401 note J Mazeaud.

52  Civ.[3] 26 avril 1983 Bull.Civ. III No. 90 p. 71, Rev.droit immobilier, 1983, p. 458.

53  Civ.[1] 12 novembre 1975 et Paris 5 décembre 1975 J.C.P. 1976.II.18479 note G Viney; Civ.[1] 2 février 1982 D.1982.I.R. p. 330; Civ.[2] 5 juin

1971 Bull.Civ. II No. 204 p. 145; Civ.[2] 3
octobre 1979 J.C.P. 1980.IV p. 360, D.1980
p. 325 1ère espèce, observ. G Durry,
Rev.trim.dr.civ. 1980 p. 358; Civ.[2] 14 décembre
1981 Gaz.Pal. 1982 Panorama p. 150 note
F Chabas; Civ.[2] 29 avril 1982 Gaz.Pal. 1982.2e
sem Panorama p. 331 et 332; Civ.[2] 4 juin 1984
Gaz.Pal. 1984 2e sem. p. 634 note F Chabas.

54    Voir J Ghestin : Conformité et garanties n. 1,
      ..., No. 270 et, par exemple, Civ. 11 octobre
      1966, J.C.P. 1967.II.15193 note G de La
      Pradelle; Civ.[1] 22 novembre 1978 J.C.P.
      1979.II.19139 note G Viney.

55    Voir H L et J Mazeaud et F Chabas, Traité t.III,
      2e volume, 6e ed. No. 2570 et 2579; B Starck,
      D.1974 Ch. p. 157 No. 21; Y Chartier, La répara-
      tion du préjudice No. 139 et 140.

56    Voir H L et J Mazeaud et F Chabas, op.cit.
      n. 55 No. 2583 et s., 2540 et 2541; B Starck,
      Chronique précitée n. 55, D.1974 p. 157 No. 30;
      Y Chartier, op.cit. n. 55, No. 490.

57    Voir notamment Com. 20 juillet 1973 Bull.Civ. IV
      No.236 p.254; 29 janvier 1974 J.C.P. 1974.
      II.17852; Civ.[1] 5 mai 1982 D.1982, I.R. p.358;
      Civ.[3] 3 janvier 1984 J.C.P. 1984.IV p. 79. Voir
      pour cette jurisprudence, P Le Tourneau,
      article précité n. 42, Rev.trim. dr.com. 1980
      p. 231 et s.: J Ghestin : Conformité et garan-
      ties n. 1, ... No. 256; B Starck, Chronique
      précitée n. 55, D.1974 p. 157, No. 64 a 75.

58    Civ.[3] 30 octobre 1978 et Com. 6 novembre 1978,
      J.C.P. 1979.II.19178 note J Ghestin.

59    Voir J Ghestin : Conformite et garanties n. 1,
      ... No. 273 à 276.

60    On peut citer notamment à cet égard la recom-
      mandation du 27 juin 1978 sur les clauses
      abusives dans les contrats de garantie (B.O.S.P.
      du 24 février 1979), la recommandation du 23
      septembre 1980 sur les contrats d'achat d'objets
      d'ameublement (B.O.C.C. due 26 novembre 1980) et
      la recommandation du 28 octobre 1980 concernant
      les delais de livraison (B.O.S.P. 26 novembre
      1980). Voir également les autres recommanda-
      tions dans la brochure éditée à la fin de
      l'annee 1985 par le Sécretariat d'Etat charge
      du Budget de la consommation : "contrats :
      attention aux clauses abusives".

61    Voir J Revée : La prévention des accidents
      domestiques; Vers un régime spécifique de
      responsabilité du fait des produits? D.1984 Ch.
      p. 69.

62    Loi du 12 juillet 1977 modifiée par la loi du 21
      octobre 1982 sur le contrôle des produits
      chimiques, D.85.217 du 13 janvier 1985 portant
      sur le controle des produits chimiques (D.1985
      L.200).

63    On peut également souligner ici que la loi du
      15 juillet 1975 relative a l'élimination des
      déchets et a la récuperation des matériaux fait
      obligation aux producteurs et distributeurs de
      déchets susceptibles de nuire a l'environnement
      d'assurer la disparition des risques crées par
      ces produits. Et la France a d'ailleurs propose
      de generaliser au plan international le prin-
      cipe de la responsabilité du producteur sur le
      contrôle complet de l'elimination des déchets
      toxiques (voir question écrite No. 41235
      J.O.Debats Ass.Nat. No. 10 5 mars 1984).

64    Voir J Calais Auloy : Propositions pour un
      nouveau droit de la consommation, La
      Documentation française, avril 1985, p. 185 à
      188 et le rapport explicatif p. 83 à 88.

65    Il peut s'agir de celui qui :
      "1°) soit presenté un produit comme sien en y
      apposant son nom, sa marque ou un autre signe
      distinctif,
      2°) soit importé un produit pour le mettre
      sur le marché,
      3°) soit fournit un produit dont le producteur
      ne peut etre identifié, à moins qu'il n'indique
      dans un bref delai l'identité du producteur ou
      de celui qui lui a fourni le produit."
      Et la texte ajoute qu' "en cas de dommage
      causé par un defaut du produit incorporé dans un
      autre, sont responsables le producteur de la
      partie composante et celui qui a réalisé
      l'incorporation".

66    En revanche, elle n'a pas prévu d'obligation
      d'assurance. Voir, à ce sujet, les observations
      critiques de Mlle J Revel, Chronique precitée,
      n. 1, D.1984 ch. p. 67 et s., No. 18 et 19.

67    Voir ce texte in J Calais-Auloy n. 64, Proposi-
      tions pour un nouveau droit de la consommation,
      p.175 à 180 et le rapport explicatif, p.65 à 76.

68    Mais non tout à fait identique car la sécurité
      est appreciee d'après l'attente légitime de
      toute personne qui se trouve être victime d'un
      dommage causé par le produit et non pas
      seulement du "consommateur".

69    Article 114 du projet. Voir J Calais-Auloy,
      op.cit. n. 64, p. 175.

70    Art. 115.

## PRODUCTS LIABILITY: THE WEST-GERMAN
## APPROACH

*Spiros Simitis*


1. Background

Product-related injuries are, no doubt, an international problem. The figures may vary.[1] The
necessity to cope with product-originating damages
belongs, however, to the policy problems common to
all industrialized countries. The higher in fact
the degree of industrialization, the more sophisticated the technological means, the more obvious also
the need for rules permitting us to accommodate the
risks accompanying the use of products typical for
everyday life and work in an industrialized society.
Basically, there are three possible reactions.
Damages may either be externalized by burdening them
upon the potential sufferer, internalized by providing a compensation duty of the producers or, lastly,
socialized by distributing them among certain
groups, if not the entire society.[2]

Though the options may be clear, the choice is
nevertheless complicated. A single look into the
history of products liability shows how contested
all attempts to allocate the risks have been and
still are. Surprisingly enough, most Continental
countries avoided until late into the fifties any
reference to product-related injuries as a particular problem. Since then it has of course become
quite fashionable to trace the origins of the controversy back to the beginning of the century. Thus,
Germans found glass splinters in salt packages[3] at
nearly the same time as Mr MacPherson was thrown out
of his collapsing Buick[4] and a few years before the
unfortunate Miss Donoghue opened the by now famous
ginger-beer bottle.[5] The truth, however, is, that

---

*       For footnotes see p. 123

compared to the long list of cases transforming products liability into a normal topic of all the
repertories of American jurisprudence, the number of
German, French, Swiss or Italian decisions remained
up to the fifties so small as to be unnoteworthy.
Still, at the 1968 meeting of the German Lawyers'
Association, a well-known barrister spoke of the
attempts to provide specific rules for product-
related injuries as an unjustified ,import of a
typically American "good".[6]

Both the sudden change and the criticism can be
understood only if they are seen in the context of
the far more general discussion of the protection of
consumers. The expectations for new liability standards are in fact linked to the conviction that more
attention should be paid to the consumer's particular situation and therefore a legal framework
developed, specifying and guaranteeing his interests.[7] Product-related injuries are indeed one of
the most typical examples of the risks run by consumers in an industrialized society. Consequently,
what was later called the "exploitation theory"[8]
became the dominant approach for all reflections on
the allocation of risks. Products liability is, in
other words, symptomatic of the mounting scepticism
provoked by an allocation connecting the economic
predominance of the manufacturer over the production
process with legal strategies excluding responsibility for the very results of this process. By
focusing on the consumer, the direction is reversed;
the internalization rather than the externalization
of risks becomes the target of all liability reflections. The discovery of products liability is thus
more than a new label for an old problem; it is in
fact the unmistakable signal for a radical change of
policies.

However, despite the late beginning of the
debate, the discussion followed the same old paths
cherished, for instance, by the courts in the United
States in the course of their attempts to find a
convincing legal pattern. The history of products
liability is therefore, in Germany as everywhere
else, a complicated tour leading from what at first
seemed to be a simple exercise in contracts to the
frontiers of tort law.[9]

2.   The Fiction as Refuge: the Contractual Approach

The contractual approach offers two advantages. It
permits us to operate within a traditional, well-
known frame work. Nothing appears, after all, more
normal than to consider product-related injuries as

a result of defective goods. Once, however, this is
accepted, the legal evaluation seems to present no
problem. Damages caused by defective articles are
traditionally in the first place dealt with by the
law of contracts. The seller-buyer relationship is
the typical channel for the distribution of goods on
the market. Conflicts arising out of the use of
marketable articles are therefore seen and treated
in the context of a contract to purchase goods. No
serious attempt to solve problems linked to the functions of the market can under these conditions
bypass the law of contracts. It must, on the contrary, start by analyzing the chances of a conflict
solution offered by contractual rules.

For German law there is, however, an additional
reason for favouring the contractual approach. Any
step towards an alternative allocation mechanism is
bound to lead to serious disadvantages. In contrast
to most other laws, the German civil code, while
foreseeing a vicarious liability of employers for
employees' errors (Art. 831), permits the employer
to exculpate himself by proving that he exercised
due care in the selection and supervision of his personnel. The implications for damages originating in
an industrial production process are obvious: the
restriction of liability appears to be the inescap-
able consequence of the division of labour. The very
moment the employer establishes an organization with
a view to producing certain goods, he reduces his
responsibility. However, a rule thought to be a
necessary tool for an accelerated industrialization
becomes a major obstacle as soon as the law is en-
trusted with the task of compensating damages due to
industrial products. A liability understood as an
internalization of risks is incompatible with an
exculpation of the producer.

Therefore, as long as the tort rules do not facilitate compensation, the courts are, understandably
enough, tempted to stick to the contractual
approach. The price is, however, high. A series of
concessions substantially altering the structure of
contract law has to be made. Product-related
injuries do not fit into the scheme of a strictly bi-
partite conflict. They constantly involve, as experience shows, persons neither bound by nor interested
in the contractual relationship. Even if the privity concept is interpreted very broadly, it is still
impossible to disregard totally the contractual
bonds and to include all injured persons, at least
as long as warranties are understood as the result
of a personal agreement and not of the simple use of
a good.

Besides, manufacturers may, as the case of the automobile industry shows, extend their organization to both the production and the distribution process; a direct relationship between the producer and the user is nevertheless not the rule. Even if the retail seller is deeply influenced by the technical knowledge and the economic impact of the producer, the goods reach the user through a separate organization, pursuing its own tasks and, at least legally, clearly distinguished from the producer. The contractual relationship is therefore situated outside the real risk zone. It comes into existence at a point where the conditions for the injuries have already been set.

Finally, the law of contracts derives its justification from the ability of the parties to adapt the rules governing their relationship to their specific expectations and particular interests. Both the courts and the legislator may therefore establish certain liability principles: ultimately, however, they offer only a possible pattern of behaviour intended to help the parties in finding an acceptable solution but not to substitute their view of the compensation modalities. To move, therefore, into the field of contracts means accepting liability standards eliminating virtually every protection granted either by statute or by court decisions. Contracting out is not an abnormal consequence but a normal implication of a conflict solving mechanism deliberately rejecting any regulatory intereference.

Clearly, none of these problems has been ignored. On the contrary, the reaction of German courts reflects the general tendency to uphold the contractual approach with the help of rules maximizing the flexibility of the law of contracts. The courts have thus, for instance, considerably extended the number of persons protected by contractual remedies by modifying the *ius quaesitum tertio*. In most of the product-related injury cases the contract between the manufacturer and the wholesale dealer is the starting point of a chain of agreements under which the product is processed to the ultimate users. The *ius quaesitum tertio* served, therefore, as the orientation mark for what was called a contract with protective effect on third parties.[10] Whoever sells one of the current consumer products is, it is thought, in no other position than, for example, a landlord. In both cases the contract deals with goods, the use of which is by no means limited to the party having entered the contract. At least the family members will have

access to the flat and, of course, to the dish-
washer, the vacuum-cleaner, and the mineral-water
bottles. Consequently, the foreseeable use by third
parties is transformed first into a duty to protect
them from possible damages and then into a contractual right of action against the manufacturer stemming out of his agreement with the wholesaler.

Another, no less ingenious, way of sidestepping
the privity obstacle was the sudden discovery of
implied warranties. Manufacturers tend indeed, notwithstanding the lack of a direct relationship with
the potential users, to address them openly, either
through marketing strategies deliberately aiming at
the consumer's expectations or through the explicitly assumed obligation to perform all necessary
repairs. The consumer relies therefore upon a
series of expectations created by the manufacturer.
Thus, behind the formal contract with the retailer
there is a second, by far more important, *de facto*
relationship with the producer, built upon the trust
in the qualities of the product and the manufacturer's readiness to correct possible defects.
The advantage is obvious: the buyer can claim
damages directly from the manufacturer, and is no
longer forced to use his contractual bonds with the
retailer as an operational basis.

Moreover, implied warranties force, at least at
first, the manufacturer to give up his best means of
self-defence: contracting-out. But, once the tendency to establish a direct relationship accompanied
by a compensation duty becomes apparent, manufacturers react quickly. Instead, for instance, of
limiting themselves to a simple description of the
product as well as to instructions for its use they
add a single phrase excluding all doubts about the
refusal to assume responsibility for product-related
injuries.

For the courts, however, this is a comparatively easy obstacle. By using such clauses, the
manufacturer opens the way for an application of the
rules on standard contracts. The courts can, in
other words, eliminate the restriction of liability
by referring to the control mechanisms developed in
a view of the standardization of agreements, an attitude particularly justified by the fact that the purpose is in both cases identical: a better protection
of the consumer.

It is, of course, not difficult to uncover a
whole series of points demonstrating the inconsist-
ency as well as the inefficiency of all attempts to

ensure a purely contractual approach.[11] Whose use of the product is, for instance, really "foreseeable" in order to admit a "special" relationship with the producer; and why is it justifiable to compensate the damages of the purchaser's wife but to deny any help to the guest of the family having used the same hairdryer or having had the misfortune to be the first to open the famous exploding bottle? Besides, what happens to bystanders in the case of an implied warranty? They never had it in mind to establish any kind of contract with the manufacturer of the particular car that most unfortunately hit them while they were peacefully walking home. No wonder, therefore, that the courts rather quickly abandoned the field to a few academics still convinced of the applicability of the contractual approach.

The importance of the controversies over each of these details should, however, not be overestimated. By far more interesting are the general implications of the proposed remedies for the law of contracts. Superficially, the allocation of production risks is achieved through the traditional channels of a purely contractual regulation. But as a matter of fact, none of the means used corresponds to the elementary expectations of the law of contracts. The manufacturer has at no point declared his willingness to cover the damages of a virtually unlimited number of persons. Nor was he prepared to warrant that his products were really free of any defects. His only undisputable intention is shown by those contract clauses which openly shift all risks to the potential user. What therefore happens behind an apparently untouched contract front is a deliberate use of contractual instruments for purposes absolutely contrary to the very principles of the law of contracts. Not the parties but the courts define the content of the agreement. The relationship between the manufacturer and the buyer of the products is, therefore, not governed by the expectations guiding the formulation of the agreements but by the intentions the producer should, according to the courts, have had. "Tacit" or "implied" warranties have nothing whatsoever to do with the manufacturer's views, but very much to do with the courts understanding of a "reasonable" allocation of risks.

There are certainly good reasons for the sometimes far too obvious accumulation of fictions. In a legal system accepting the predominance of contractual regulations, the fictitious intentions of the parties confer an assumption of legality on the mandatory regime developed by judicial interference.

The "tacit" warranty is still a warrranty based on
an assumed decision of the parties justified by the
attempt to redress a balance of interests otherwise
reached through a bargaining process. For many
observers, but also for the courts, there could
therefore be no doubt that by reinterpreting the contract the judiciary was still sticking to the principles enunciated nearly a century ago by the Cour
de Cassation[12] and defining the judges as faithful
executors of the parties' intentions. The question,
however, is, whether historically understandable
legitimacy strategies must be upheld in a system no
longer characterized by the supremacy of the
individual will but by the adaption of individual
behaviour to an increasingly refined set of rules
set by an activist state and court machinery.

3.    The Delictual Action: A First Step Towards
      Strict Liability

The German courts rather quickly abandoned all
attempts at a contractual approach and chose to deal
with products liability as a tort problem. In fact,
shortly after the 1968 meeting of the German
Lawyers' Association[13] and only two years after its
first decision on product-related injuries, the
Supreme Federal Court[14] openly stated its preference
for the rules provided by the law of torts. The
court, of course, phrased its decision in habi-
tually cautious judicial language. The decision
does not simply reject the use of contractual instruments once and for all, but states that there may be
exceptional situations in which liability has to be
judged according to contractual standards.[15]
Nevertheless, the court's position is unequivocal:
the Supreme Court is not prepared to tolerate the
usual fictions. When it therefore speaks of the
possibility of a contractual approach, it means and
expects an agreement covered by the explicit
intention of the parties.

     The priority given to the delictual action may
permit the abandonment of widespread fictions, but it
does not automatically solve all problems. On the
contrary, at least two serious obstacles remain. The
first has already been mentioned: article 831 of the
Civil Code. Liability is no more than a pure
academic exercise as long as the producer can simply
point to the proper care he exercised in the
selection and supervision of his employees.

     Damages lead certainly back to the behaviour of
the employees involved in the production process.
To personalize the cause of damage amounts, at least

at first, to a switch of the responsibility from the manufacturer to his personnel. Once, therefore, the judges clearly opted for a delictual action their next move had to be a careful circumvention of Article 831. Probably the easiest way is to reconsider the onus of proof. Instead of asking the injured person to describe a production process, not only unknown to him but also deliberately kept secret with the help of both organizational measures and legal regulations, in order to unveil its deficiencies, the manufacturer was faced with the obligation to localize the source of injury and to explain what steps had been taken in advance to diminish the possible risks for future users. In other words, as long as the manufacturer is unable to offer a satisfactory explanation there is no alternative to liability.

Behind the reversed onus of proof there is more than a simple reconsideration of traditional procedural rules. The Supreme Court, in fact, opens the way for a liability concept adapted to the specific structure of entrepreneurial activity.[16] The reflections on the burden of proof are linked to a careful distinction between the possible reasons for the product-related injury. For the courts there are at least four quite different causes: manufacturing faults, design faults, faulty instructions and development risks.[17]

Manufacturing faults have clearly limited consequences. The damages are due to a more or less accidental fact. The erroneous behaviour of a single employee leads to the production of one or, in the worst of all cases, of a few defective products. The damage remains thus an isolated event. Where, on the contrary, a design fault occurs, the entire production series is affected. The risk is no longer limited to the use of a single product: every purchaser, driver or passenger of a specific automobile, for instance, is endangered. The situation remains basically the same whenever faulty instructions are given. The product may as such function perfectly, but only as long as certain rules are observed. The user must therefore be informed in good time, in an unequivocal and understandable language. The defect is, in other words, to be found in a lack of communication excluding a correct appreciation of the product. Experience shows, however, that, especially in the field of pharmaceutical products, damages are often due to the use of substances considered at the time of production, in view of the then existing standards of knowledge, as harmless or at least not apt to cause the particular injuries occurring during the subsequent use. Development risks refer thus to a danger inherent in the product, but not yet discoverable.

However vague the description of the various causes may be, the classification has an undisputable advantage: it indicates the expectations of the courts. Products liability can, in the opinion of the judges, by no means be limited to the compensation of an accidental individual misbehaviour. The more the courts dealt with product-related injuries, the more they focused on the responsibility of the producer to exclude risks by an adequate organization. Only where the necessary attention is given to the organizational aspects of the entire production process, is there a sufficiently realistic chance of preventing dangers due to both defective designs and incomplete, misunderstandable, or erroneous instructions. In each of these cases the damage demonstrates in the eyes of the courts the inability of the manufacturer to respond to the demands of his specific entrepreneurial purposes by organizational means neutralizing the potential risks for the future product user.

What the courts therefore did, was to establish a particular entrepreneurial duty based on the acknowledgement of the risks accompanying the production and aiming at an allocation of these risks according to the power and the opportunities to interfere with the only decisive source of damage: the production process. The advantage is twofold. On the one hand the courts have no longer to worry about provisions like Art. 831 of the Civil Code. The organizational duty attaches the responsibility directly to the producer. Whether the damage was caused by a defective machine, momentary carelessness of an employee, the poor equipment of the research department or the unwillingness of the sales manager to spend enough money on a precise description of the product and its potential dangers is irrelevant. Neither the users nor the courts need to enter the perilous way of localizing the cause of damage. The mere fact of a product-related damage is quite sufficient to raise the one and only important question, whether the producer has fulfilled his organizational duty. Since he is the sole addressee of the organizational expectations, it is also up to him to establish that the production process was organized in a risk-proof way. Where he fails to prove that concrete steps had been taken in order to avoid the specific damages, the lack of adequate organizational measures has to be compensated by a redress of the injuries.

On the other hand, the organizational duty permits an acceptable compromise with the leading principle of tort law. Liability is the price of the
failure to fulfil an obligation incumbent on all
manufacturers. They must, in other words, bear the
consequences of their fault and are therefore
treated in exactly the same way as any other person
exercising an activity causing damage. The organizational duty enables the judges to stay within the
field of a tort system dominated by the fault principle. The courts can claim to have successfully
reacted to the threats caused by a highly industrialized production process without questioning the
traditional allocation rule. The organizational
duty thus innovates and pacifies at the same time.
It allows the field of application of the existing
rules to extend, but also evokes the impression that
the cornerstone of tort law, the requirement of
fault, is still the decisive allocation criterion.[18]

However, what at first looks rather convincing
is ultimately at best a provisory escape from the
liability problems. The assumed compatibility with
the fault principle is in fact a mere fiction.
Through the fault principle the legislator introduced a clearly subjective element into the evaluation process for the allocation of damages. The
idea that the mere injury of certain fundamental
elements of individual activity (like property,
life or health) should be entirely sufficient to
justify a compensation claim was openly rejected.
Tort law asked for more than simple damage; it
demanded a moral condemnation. The importance
attached to fault is the answer to this expectation.
Liability can be admitted because the injury is
imputable to a particular person in view of a
morally unacceptable behaviour. The moral dis-
qualification reflects, however, more than a political and philosophical concept viewing societal
development as the result of sovereign individual
decisions. It is a deliberate legal contribution to
the expanding industry. The more the manufacturer
can reduce his liability, the better the chances for
an increased investment in industrial production.
The externalization of production costs establishes
market priorities and grants privileges to the
manufacturer at the expense of the potential user.
Any reflection on the repartition of damages leads
therefore inevitably to a discussion of the economic
and political principles governing the production as
well as the distribution of goods.

Consequently, as long as the fault principle
remains the leading rule of tort liability, alloca-

tion decisions have to take into consideration the personal attitude of the tortfeasor. However, organizational demands, once taken seriously, eliminate gradually all subjective elements. In at least three of the already mentioned four main groups of injury causes there can be no case where the damages could not have been prevented by specific measures. The question can therefore only be, whether the fault principle requires at least some concessions to the particular subjective aspects of the production process, if, for instance, a fault must be denied whenever the manufacturer invested the subjectively adequate amount of capital and acted according to the personally available and applicable technical means. None of the courts was obviously prepared to follow such reasoning. They on the contrary insisted on a purely objective standard of care. The personal resources were not considered as decisive but rather the demands based on the newest stage of technical development. The consequences can be easily described: manufacturers must either comply with an objective standard, irrespective of their personal means and capacities, or abandon the intended economic activity. The organisational duty amounts thus to a liability strictly based on an objective evaluation of the production process and therefore an equally objective allocation of damages. Due to the high expectations of the courts, manufacturers have virtually no chance to escape liability. In sum, the courts bypass, with the help of the organizational duty, the fault principle and open the way for a strict liability.

It can, of course, be argued that the deliberate choice of rules contradicting the established liability system is the unavoidable price for an allocation protecting the user. A careful analysis of the various cases shows, however, that the courts are by no means willing to shift the risks unconditionally. They in fact refrain from admitting a compensation duty as soon as the most critical and controversial area is reached: the development risk. The unwillingness to extend the manufacturer's liability is understandable. In every other case the fiction of a fault can at least be preserved. But where the damage is due to conditions unforeseeable even by the most sophisticated and advanced technical procedures, no court can earnestly pretend to operate under a fault regime. Any attempt to secure compensation amounts to an open abandonment of the fault principle. What otherwise can be hidden behind the assumed duty of the manufacturer to organize the production process in a risk-free way is no more feasible when it comes to development risks. Where, because of a still unknown source of injury, no adequate measures can be taken, there can also be no duty of the manufacturer to stop an ongoing but undetectable damage process.

The dilemma of the courts may be obvious; the consequences for the product users are no less clear. In the most dangerous cases the compensation chances are irrevocably lost. One has only to remember the damages due to the use of pharmaceuticals in order to realize what an externalization means for the potential users. They and not the producer have to bear the consequences of an innovatory procedure initiated and pursued exclusively by the manufacturer. The latter is thus able to experiment without having to cover the injuries caused by his products. Liability can, of course, be established as soon as the first damages occur and the manufacturer persists in distributing his product.[19] But experience shows how difficult it is to fix the exact moment from which the risk is shifted. Drugs often remain on the market as long as their negative effects have not reached a stage at which the manufacturer is convinced that a compensation duty has become unavoidable.

Besides, in a highly industrialized society development risks are the really crucial point for all attempts to establish rules protecting the user. Because of the mass character of production and of the increasingly subtilized marketing strategies the probability of widespread damage affecting a larger number of persons is high. Neither are development risks restricted to a few pharmaceutical products intended for a small group of patients suffering from rare diseases; nor are carcinogenic substances to be found only in a very limited amount of products used under exceptional conditions. The asbestos cases, as well as the experiences with paint-on wood preservatives, demonstrate clearly that development risks are part of the dangers accompanying the use of everyday products by perfectly normal consumers in equally perfectly normal situations. The credibility of products liability rules depends, therefore, to a decisive extent on their ability to ensure a convincing allocation of damages for development risks. As long as compensation is avoided, any solution offered remains incomplete and provisory.

The more, however, purely objective standards are accepted the less understandable the attitude of the courts becomes. Once they started abandoning an allocation system obviously favouring the manu-

facturer the next step should have been to adopt
openly rules ensuring an adequate protection of the
potential users instead of operating in a field full
of contradictions. Any such move would ultimately
have led to a judicial revision of the tort
liability principles, in fact to an unequivocal
replacement of the fault-bound allocation by a
compensation system disregarding any responsibility
of the manufacturer in the conventional sense. This
would, not only in the opinion of the courts, have
gone far beyond a simple redistribution of losses.
For nearly a century the fault principle was presented as the result of a binding legislative decision. No one but the legislator was and is, according to the still prevailing opinion, entitled to
establish exceptions. Consequently, it was the legislator who, whenever the necessity of a non-fault
liability was acknowledged, from traffic accidents
to nuclear risks, laid down the condition under
which compensation has to be provided. Any reference to an alternative liability system is thus, at
least in German law, linked to a series of particular cases having deliberately been treated in a
specific way on the basis of previous legislative
decisions.

There is certainly no question that the change
of policy necessitated for a long time a legislative
action. The Civil Code's preference for a fault-
bound compensation was all too clear. Besides, the
first doubts were indeed raised in the context of
specific conflicts. While, in other words, the
Civil Code dealt with torts in general, the revision
of the fault principle was seen and discussed as a
consequence of particular new risks due, for
instance, to rail or air traffic. What, therefore,
was questioned was not the fault principle as such
but its application in a few delimited situations.
Neither the courts nor the legislator were thus
ready to give up the fault principle. On the
contrary, they were persuaded that fault should
still be considered as an essential condition of
liability and consequently at best prepared to
tolerate some exceptions.

However, parallel to the legislative action
establishing a no-fault liability, the courts modified the interpretation of tort liability. Under the
cover of increasingly detailed standards of conduct
they developed rules minimizing and ultimately
eliminating all subjective elements. Instead of
concentrating on the individual aspects of the
tortfeasor's behaviour, the courts judged his activity exclusively on the basis of abstract objective

criteria. The failure to comply with these
standards became the sole decisive test of
liability. Thus, the fault principle was discreetly
abandoned.

The standards of conduct illustrate in what an
intricate position the courts are. They realize the
necessity to adopt new criteria for large and important parts of the tort cases. The once dominating
motive, the support of an expanding industry, is
replaced by the increasing insight into the
implications of industrialization. The allocation
of damages is therefore primarily seen as a means to
redress the imbalance between a production process
generating additional risks by the use of new
substances and methods and consumers deprived of all
chances to influence or control the sources of
damage. The courts are, in other words, not
prepared to characterize the risks as a regrettable
but unavoidable consequence of the production
process. So, instead of sticking to the fault
principle, they opt for a distribution of losses
imposing a compensation duty on whoever initiates
the risk-generating activity. But they at the same
time consider themselves bound by the legislative
history of tort liability. A direct acceptance of a
no-fault compensation is consequently seen as a
challenge to the legitimacy of judicial power.[20]

Thus, even if the self-restraint has its price
in terms of the credibility of the allocation, the
courts are prepared to accept the disadvantages of
the compromise as an inevitable tribute to the legislator's privilege to establish the policy rules.
Again: there can be no doubt that little, if anything, was left of the original liability model. The
reversal of the burden of proof, combined with
strictly objective criteria for the appreciation of
the manufacturer's behaviour, demolished the allocation system adopted by the Civil Code. But the
facade was kept intact. The courts can thus act contrary to the Civil Code provisions and still pretend
to respect them. Products liability is one more
striking example of the activist role of the courts
within legal systems nominally restraining the judiciary to the interpretation of legislative decisions
but in reality tolerating a continuous review of
legislative rules.

4.   Responsibility for Pharmaceuticals: A Model for
     Enterprise Liabiity

Judicial self-restraint is a viable regulatory principle as long as the legislator is able and willing

to react to a changing social structure by modifying
the existing laws. Judicial abstinence, even in a
very relative sense, presupposes, therefore, a learn-
ing legislative system. Where, however, as in the
case of products liability, the courts exhaust the
arsenal of fictions and increasingly suffer from a
loss of credibility, the reluctance of the legislator to interfere and to take clear decisions becomes
more and more evident. Faced with a conflict deeply
involving fundamental economic and societal interests, the legislator chooses to let the judiciary
solve problems. The advantages are obvious: not
only is the legislator relieved of the burden of
decision, the responsibility for the solutions
adopted is shifted entirely to the courts. They and
not parliament are to blame.

Experience shows nevertheless that there are
limits to the strategy of inactivity. Where widespread, spectacular damages lead to a growing public
discontent, the legislator cannot simply stick to
his abstentionist attitude. Significantly enough,
West Germany's parliament responded in a single
instance to the quest for product-liability rules:
in the case of pharmaceuticals. The thalidomide
experience had left deep traces. Though, after long
and painful litigation, a settlement had been
reached, the dramatic confrontation with the risks
accompanying the use of pharmaceutical products had
clearly demonstrated the necessity to reconsider the
allocation of damages. The injuries caused by thalidomide were not seen as a unique event but as a
symptom of radically changed conditions of production and consumption. The litigation had sufficiently demonstrated the limits of judicial
interference and the inadmissibility of a further
postponement of legislative action. The 1976 law on
drugs reflects the inevitable concession to a public
demand for a reassessment of the allocation of
damages. The reaction is, of course, limited to a
specific, particularly damage-prone sector. But the
law is nevertheless a first contribution to a new
allocation scheme. Probably its most remarkable
feature is the insight into the limited importance
of liability rules. Even the most sophisticated
user-oriented model can offer no more than monetary
compensation. However, in view of the injuries due
to pharmaceutical products, the task of the law
cannot be confined to securing the victims whatever
amount of money, but must provide mechanisms to
prevent damages as much as possible. The risk must
be avoided and not only compensated.

It is therefore not surprising that the long-forgotten, even openly rejected, punitive aspect of liability rules was revived in the course of the discussion of products liability.[21] The phrasing was, no doubt, extremely careful, the aim nevertheless obvious: a particularly high compensation sum should both punish in an exemplary way and deter from risky production methods. But the fall-back into a past period of liability rules not only grossly overestimates the impact of compensation: it also leads to nearly unsolvable problems whenever, as in the case of megadamages, very different, legitimate indemnity expectations collide.

Consequently, the West German legislator refused to identify prevention with higher compensation. He instead focused on measures directly interfering with the production process. Drugs can reach the market only after a series of clearly defined conditions has been fulfilled, from a general licence preceding any form of production, specified test demands, a special licence for the sale of a particular drug and a strict prohibition of production whenever the product may, in view of the latest scientific findings, cause damage. Liability is thus reduced to an auxiliary function. Compensation is only needed for those cases where the regulatory system was unable to prevent the damage .

At the same time the traditional approach to compensation is replaced by a no-fault liability. The pharmaceutical enterprise has to compensate all damage connected with the development or the production of drugs. There are of course exceptions and limits. The damage must, for instance, exceed the injuries "tolerable" according to the standards of medical science. In addition, the compensation duty is restricted to a specific sum. The law, nevertheless, establishes the first unequivocal case of a no-fault enterprise liability. The mere fact that the use of a drug caused injuries suffices to hold the producing enterprise responsible. The law is neither interested in the particular circumstances of production, nor does it ask at any point whether the enterprise was using its own substances or materials provided by other firms. Whoever assumes the function of either producing or supplying patients with medicines is liable for all damages they may lead to. Responsibility is thus the reverse side of production. Once the decision for an enterpreneurial activity in the pharmaceutical sector has been taken, the unconditional submission to a combined regime of preventive and compensatory rules is the necessary consequence.

However, cases like the thalidomide-related birth defects show that compensation presupposes more than an explicit duty. The legislator must also secure funds guaranteeing an adequate indemnity. Liability is always a question of solvency and for this reason realistic only if its consequences are calculated in time and dealt with by specific regulations providing for sufficient economic resources. The law therefore explicitly states that the pharmaceutical enterprise has to take the necessary measures in order to cover possible damages either through insurance or with the help of a bank guarantee.

An elaborate system of risk prevention, no-fault liability, and a secured damage coverage are thus the decisive elements of the reallocation of risks. The reflections on the compensation rules may have been the first step towards a regulation alleviating the user from the production risks. They are, nevertheless, ultimately only one of a series of regulatory instruments permitting an efficient control of the implications of the production process. Thus, there is at least one thing that can be learned from the new law: the real issue is by no means confined to a change of liability principles. The details may and will certainly vary from product to product, but a regulatory mechanism consisting of the different elements included in the Pharmaceutics Act remains the essential condition of a working protection.

5.  Policy Problems

Discussions on products liability generally convey the impression that, notwithstanding the differences of opinion, the manufacturer's responsibility has by now been acknowledged. All further reflections seem therefore to have no other aim than to clear details, A close look at the case material shows, however, that for at least five reasons products liability problems, strange as it may sound, have become even more complicated than they were at the beginning of a seemingly quite satisfactory development.

(a)  The Notion of a "Product". The reassessment of the allocation of damages was, and is still seen as, a necessary reaction to risks typically inherent both in the manufacturing and the distribution process of industrial products. However, the notion of "product" has proved to be ambiguous in at least two respects. The first is because of the tendencies to include agricultural products  -  for

many a rather astonishing expectation. In reality
it is a natural consequence of the structural
changes in agricultural production. Both the
mechanization and rationalization are late but
thorough repetitions of the industrialization
process. What therefore for a long time seemed to
be only appropriate as long as industrial products
were at stake, appears to be equally adequate in the
case of agricultural products. But the hope for a
common regulation vanishes as soon as damage sources
typical for agricultural production, like pollution,
are carefully considered. Allocation can obviously
not simply follow the pattern developed for
industry. In a certain sense the experience with
pharmaceuticals is repeated. The clearer the
differences between the various "products" to be
dealt with become, the less satisfactory abstract
compensation rules tend to be. There may exist
perfectly convincing general policy rules for
products liability. An efficient regulation
presupposes reactions deliberately taking into
account the particular aspects of both the
production process and the use of the different
categories of products. Not in the sense of
creating obstacles in order to exclude all
responsibility of producers - an impression often
conveyed by the remarks made in the course of the
discussions on the different international documents
- but in view of a really working regulation.

A second, no less intriguing, experience is the
attempt to include the so-called "negative products".[22] In fact, whoever asks for measures ensuring a risk-free industrial production implicitly
addresses the problem of waste. Once more the production process is evidently the potential source of
grave damage as the increasingly intensive demands
for enviromental protection show. No wonder therefore that at least some courts applied the products
liability standards to waste production.[23] In both
cases the manufacturer creates risks inevitably
linked to the industrial production. Consequently it
seems perfectly correct to observe the same allocation principles. The question is, however, whether
such tendencies do not irrevocably blur the conditions and limits of products liability. The mere
fact that the production process leads to certain
results cannot be sufficient for establishing uniform rules. The credibility as well as the efficiency of the proposed solutions depend primarily on
the ability to distinguish between the different
conflicts and to present answers carefully adapted
to their structure.

Even if, therefore, the production process generates the risks in each of these cases, there is no necessity for a single answer. "Negative products" have their own problems context and should for this reason be considered separately in view of a regulation taking into account the specific allocation problems created by pollution and situated thus within the framework of reflections on environmental protection. It may very well be that at the end an interdependence of products liability and environmental protection must be admitted and dealt with, but this can only be the result of an analysis clearly differentiating and not operating under the same abstract premises.

(b) The Notion of a "Producer". No less ambiguous is the notion of producer. The cases show that the injured user finds himself confronted with an increasing number of potential "producers" and is thus involved in a most intricate process of a correct choice of defendant and an adequate repartition of the compensation duty. The original assumption, that behind the product there is always one manufacturer using his own materials and applying his own methods in order to present his own products, has from the very beginning been a pure fiction, reflecting an understanding of industrial activity essentially based on a nineteenth century craft-oriented concept of the production process. The manufacturer integrates into this process a whole series of experiences, procedures and substances often developed at different places by the most different enterprises. "His" product is nearly always the result of a synthetic work.[24] Besides, in an economy operating within an international market a large part of the products are imported.[25] Finally, the example of detergents and trade-marks shows that no satisfactory analysis of the risks can omit the role sellers and retailers play.

Under these circumstances the task can only consist in reducing complexity by chanelling liability. But, when it comes to a concentration of the compensation duty, the aversion is obvious. Consequently, the user is presented with a choice reflecting most of the time the particularities of the production and distribution process. A product-oriented allocation must, however, establish clear priorities by attaching responsibility to the closest connection to the final product and avoiding, in the interest of the potential user, a fractionation of the claim. As long as this condition is not fulfilled, the user risks becoming the victim of a constant reallocation of responsibility. A

channelling of the compensation duty does not
of course, affect the internal repartition of
damage payments. To what extent payments can be
burdened upon whom depends ultimately on the
organization of the production process.

Nevertheless, even if the necessity of establishing priorities is fully admitted, the task
remains extremely difficult. The more it becomes
evident that, in order to secure compensation, none
of the different ways of making the product available to the market can be ignored, the less clear
the notion of "producer" appears to be. But because
of the ambivalence of one of the basic elements of
any allocation system for production risks, both the
credibility and the efficiency of a liability regulation are again at stake. The confusion is well illustrated by a series of decisions of the Supreme
Federal Court. For the judges there is still no
doubt that importers are by no means "producers".[26]
On the other hand, the court did, despite its own
strategies to evade Art. 831 of the Civil Code, not
hesitate to qualify managers as "producers".[27] A
last, no less significant, example are the incon-
sistant remarks in the case of "self-progressing"
defects, in other words, defects consecutively
affecting materials supplied by different
producers.[28]

(c) Products Liability Regulation. However, probably the most disturbing experience is the radical
change of functions of a products liability regulation. Documents like the directive of the European
Community still present products liability as one of
the main means for an efficient consumer protection.
But the gap between the assumed justification and
the judicial practice is deep. In fact, the very
first of the German Supreme Federal Court decisions
reversing the burden of proof, and thus outlining a
special regime for products liability,[29] had nothing
to do with what commonly is understood as consumer
protection. The action was raised by a farmer
against a pharmaceutical company. He claimed compensation for damages due to a vaccine against fowl
pest. Both parties were, in other words, entre-
preneurs and the purpose of the litigation was to
restitute damages caused by one commercial firm to
another equally commercial enterprise. The producer
of poultry sued the manufacturer of vaccines. Since
then, nothing has changed. On the contrary, the
decisions clearly demonstrate that products
liability is by now an instrument increasingly used
by producers in order to redress their damages.[30]
Consequently, none of the courts ever delimited the

potential claimants. The really decisive fact is thus not a qualification of the user but the causation of the damage by a product.[31]

The attitude of German courts is by no means unique. Despite the frequent references to the "consumer" judges rarely have attempted to draw a line between normal consumer uses and uses for business purposes. The few American decisions[32] pointing to the policy of products liability, to protect those who otherwise could not protect themselves, were quickly forgotten. There are certainly good excuses. Most laws carefully avoid a precise description of the "consumers". What they offer instead is either a specific regulation for clearly delimited conflicts in connection with specific forms of sales, where indeed business and consumer activities can be distinguished, or they try to restrict compensation to a few damages, for example purely bodily injuries, and thus indirectly exclude business interests. But distinctions like the latter are utterly unconvincing. If the purpose is to protect a certain group of persons they and not the kind of injuries they suffered are essential.

Even if, therefore, the difficulties in defining the persons entitled to sue are obvious, they do not justify the readiness to accept a regulation abandoning any distinction. Each of the decisive elements of protective rules, from the preventive measures to a no-fault liability, was developed against the background of a conflict model that explicitly focused on the position of non-commercial users, from the buyer of typical consumer goods to the injured bystander. Commercial enterprises have, no doubt, their problems with defective products, and it is certainly not always easy to distinguish between a purely personal and a commercial use, as the example of defective cars shows. But again, the question is, whether in view of these difficulties a development radically reversing the original intentions should be tolerated.

Products liability has thus reached a crucial point. The courts operate, to put it bluntly, under false premises. While still pretending to have the consumer in mind, they enrich the arsenal of business litigation. If therefore products liability is in a crisis, then it is because of this development and not on account of the sums adjudicated or the delimitation of damages. However, most criticisms of the compensation rules concentrate on the details rather than on questioning whether they really reflect a consumer-based regulation.[33] Interestingly

enough, the initial opposition to products liability has largely faded. Specific insurance
policies have certainly reduced the resistance on
the part of industry.[34] But once it became clear
that the compensation duty can be instrumentalized
for business purposes the liability was no longer cate-
gorically rejected. The attention shifted instead
to the conditions guaranteeing an adequate indemnity
for business damages. One more reason to ask anew
for an unequivocal justification of a liability
scheme with precise aims : to trace, in other words,
the way back from a non-committal attachment to the
product damage to a policy-oriented definition of
the persons entitled to sue.

(d) Economic Losses. The restitution of economic
losses is still one of the most controversial
points. In fact, products liability was and is seen
as a means to compensate life or property injuries,
to a great extent the result of the unanimous
opinion that products liability claims must be
distinguished from all legal instruments securing
quality expectations. Besides, under laws like the
German Civil Code, economic losses are not covered
by tort liability. However, the courts have, long
before products liability was first discussed, in
order to ensure a better protection of business
interests, interpreted the Civil Code provisions in
a way permitting a recovery of economic losses;
property and the ongoing business were simply
equated.[35]

But, despite its intensity, the controversy
misses the real issue. A correct evaluation of the
restitution of economic losses depends on the
knowledge of the conflicts to be solved with the
help of the liability rules. As long as any delimitation of the potential claimants is avoided and
the compensation claim consequently seen as a legal
means available for business purposes, economic
losses not only play a predominant role, they also
change drastically the financial implication of
products liability. The simplest way to reduce substantially the amount of damages to be paid is under
these conditions a clear denial of any restitution
obligation as far as economic losses are concerned.
Once, however, the application field of the liability rules is narrowed by excluding business uses,
there is no convincing reason for a restrictive
treatment of pecuniary or other losses. Compensation
must aim at a full recovery irrrespective of whether
there has been a bodily injury or an economic loss.
Instead, therefore, of looking for indirect ways to
justify a payment,[36] by qualifying, for instance,

the economic losses as a damage related to the
personal injury, the restitution duty should be
openly admitted. There is certainly a grey area
within which compensation may be used in order to
substitute or to expand remedies for lacking
quality. But any attempt to inhibit such tendencies
must exclusively focus on this particular problem
and not convert it into an argument eliminating all
compensation of economic losses.[37]

(e) Damages. No discussion of products liability
can nevertheless ignore the size of damages. Figures
and arguments should, however, be considered
carefully, especially in the context of a comparative analysis. American law, for example, was and
is one of the main sources of information whenever
liability models are considered. But while in the
fifties and sixties the American experience was
invoked in order to demonstrate the necessity of
regulations, references to the American cases have
by now the opposite function: they are used as an
argument for a restriction of products liability.[38]
Like in the United States, paradoxical cases as well
as the often astonishing amount of compensation
claimed, are regarded as unmistakable signs of the
lack of any economic rationality and as a proof of
the wisdom of the traditional provisions.[39] However,
neither the size of the claims, nor the often indeed
rather strange cases, can be understood without
taking into consideration the American jury system
as well as the admissibility of contingent fees.
Where, like for instance in West Germany, none of
these conditions is present, similar experiences
cannot occur. What therefore is really needed is
not an abstract analysis of the compensation rules
but a precise discussion of the implications of both
the jury system and of contingent fees for products
liability.

Yet another set of arguments loses much of its
plausibility, once it is looked at from a
comparative standpoint. Any move towards strict
liability must, according to a widespread view, be
necessarily accompanied by a clear delimitation of
the compensation sum. Under cover of alleged
necessity, both the producers and the insurers have
attempted to erect an additional barrier against an
unwanted compensation duty. It is indeed correct
that, especially in Germany, strict liability has
generally been linked to provisions fixing a
specific maximum amount. But this is, in no way,
even for German law a *conditio sine qua non* and can
certainly not be presented as a universally
admitted, binding principle. For water damages, for

instance, West German law foresees no limits whatsoever[40] and as far as other countries are concerned
it has been repeatedly and sufficiently demonstrated
that no such thing as a general rule imposing a
limitation exists.[41]

But especially when all attempts to limit the
compensation sum are rejected, the long-term implications of liability must be carefully considered. The
purpose of a regulation cannot simply be to
establish liability, it must also make sure that
there is a realistic chance of compensation. This
is why the already mentioned West German law on
pharmaceuticals asks for coverage. However, damages
due to the use of industrial products are by no
means the sole risk created by a constantly
developed and intensified industrial production. The
implications for the labour market as well as the
environmental consequences indicate two other, no
less important, risk factors. Both are at the same
time examples of additional, equally significant compensation duties. The West German legislator has,
for instance, not only attempted to guarantee
employees at least a minimum compensation whenever
the existence of the enterprise is economically
endangered, but also gradually increased responsibility for environmental damages.

The result can, particularly whenever megadamages occur, easily be a collision between the
different compensation duties. The experiences with
the thalidomide as well as the asbestos cases demonstrate the dilemma. Consequently, exhaustive compensation of all product-related or environmental
damages may endanger both the position of the
workers and of the product-users. The cumulation of
duties compels us, therefore, to re-examine carefully the conditions and the limits of an internalization of damages and to consider the possibility of establishing priorities. Insurance may to
some extent offer a solution. But still, the
question cannot be avoided, whether at least certain
risks should be externalized, in other words compensated through the individual insurance of the potential victims, or at least partly socialized. To be
clear: the eventual consequences of a cumulation are
by no means an argument permitting us to contest
successfully a regulation of the risks accompanying
the production process. They stress, however, the
necessity to be constantly conscious of the interdependence of the various obligations. If, therefore,
products liability is to be understood as a typical
case of enterprise liability, then the final answer
to all questions concerning the conditions and the

content of the indemnity can be given only after having considered the interconnections with all the
other compensation duties related to the enterprise
activity and their common implications for both the
structure of the firm and the indemnification of the
potential claimants.

## FOOTNOTES

1   See for West Germany , Schmidt-Salzer,
    Betriebs-Berater (BB) 1982, 1251 and for the
    United States, Product Safety and Liability
    Reporter (BNA) 511 (29 June, 1979).

2   For a detailed discussion see Fleming, *The Law
    of Torts* (6th ed) (1983) 6; Bruggemeier, Archiv
    für die civilistische Praxis (AcP) 182 (1982)
    385; Hastings International and Comparative Law
    Review (1983) 356.

3   Reichsgericht, Entscheidungen in Zivilsachen
    (RGZ) 87, 1.

4   *MacPherson v Buick Motor Co* 217 NY 382, 11 NE
    1050.

5   *Donoghue v Stevenson* [1932] AC 562.

6   Mohring, Verhandlungen des 47. Deutschen
    Juristentages, Nürnberg 1968, vol 2 (1968) M 69.

7   See eg Verhandlungen des 47. Deutschen
    Juristentages, Nürnberg 1968, vol 1 (1968) C 7
    et seq., 2 (1968) N 6 et seq.; K. Simitis,
    Verbraucherschutz, Schlagwort oder Rechts-
    prinzip (1976) 50; Lukes, Reform der
    Produkthaftung (1979) 13; Schwark, AcP 179
    (1979) 75.

8   Priest, 90 Yale LJ 1299 (1981).

9   For a comprehensive description see Simitis,
    Verhandlungen des 47. Deutschen Juristentages,
    Nürnberg 1968, vol 1 (168) C 7; von Marschall,
    in Deutsche Zivil-, Kollisions-und Wirtschafts-
    rechtiche Beiträge zum X. Internationalen
    Kongres fur Rechtsvergleichung in Budapest 1978
    (1978); Schmidt-Salzer, Produkthaftung (1973);
    Bruggemeier, Wertpapier-Mittellungen (WM) 1982,
    1295; Hager, AcP 184 (1984) 413.

10  See Bundesgerichtshof, Entscheidungen in Zivil-
    sachen (BGHZ) 66, 51; 69, 86; 70, 329; 75, 323.

11  Simitis, Grundfragen der Produzentenhaftung
    (1965) 27; Bruggemeier, WM 1982, 1295.

12    Cass civ 17/6/1896, Dalloz, Périodique 99.1.159.

13    Verhandlungen op cit n.7, vol 1 C 8, vol 2, M 6.

14    BGHZ 51, 91.

15    See also Bundesgerichtshof, BB 1984, 2148.

16    The products liability decisions are part of "the ongoing process of 'decodification'", Fleming, 4 Oxford Journal of Legal Studies 238.

17.   See for a detailed description Simitis, Verhandlungen op citn. 9, 35; Diederichsen, Neue Juristische Wochenschrift (NJW) 1978, 1281; Schmidt-Salzer, BB 1981, 1041; Bruggemeier, WM 1982, 1300.

18    The choice of the courts was therefore indeed "the less activist-solution", Fleming, 4 Oxford Journal of Legal Studies 240.

19    In view of the specific observation and control duty, established by the courts, BGHZ 80, 186, 199; Schmidt-Salzer, BB 1981, 1041; Hager, Versicherungsrecht 1984, 799.

20    No wonder that the courts have ignored all well-meant advice (see eg Kotz, AcP 170 (1970) 15) to establish openly a no-fault-liability. For a critical evaluation see Ficker, Festschrift für Duden (1977) 93; Simitis, Festschrift für Duden (1977) 605; Esser/Weyers, Schuldrecht Band 2: Besonderer Teil Ein Lebuch 6, neubearb. (1984) 484.

21    See Mertens, Münchener Kommentar zum Burgerlichen Gesetzbuch (1980), Introductory notes 31 et seq to 823.

22    See Bruggemeier, WM 1982, 1300.

23    Bundesgerichtshof, Versicherungsrecht 1976, 62.

24    See BGHZ 67, 359; 80, 186; 86, 256; Bundesgerichtshof, BB 1984, 2148.

25    Bundesgerichtshof, NJW 1980, 1219.

26    Bundesgerichtshof, NJW 1980, 1219.

27    Bundesgerichtshof, NJW 1975, 1827.

28    BGHZ 86, 256; Stoll, Juristenzeitung 1983, 591; Diederichsen, Versicherungsrecht 1984, 799; Kallmann, BB 1985, 409.

29    BGHZ 51, 91.

30    See for instance Bundesgerichtshof, Versicherungsrecht 1972, 149, 659; 1977, 839; 1983, 346; BGHZ 80, 186, 199; Kallmann, BB 1985, 409.

31  See also Hager, AcP 184 (1984) 419.

32  See eg *Seely v White Motor Co* 403 P 2d 145
    (1965); *Southwest Forest Industries Inc v
    Westinghouse Electric Corp.*, 422 F 2d 1013
    (1970).

33  See the controversy between Priest, 90 Yale LJ
    1297 (1981), 91 Yale L.J. 1386 (1982) and
    Whitford, 91 Yale LJ 1391 (1982).

34  For details see Das Risiko der Produkthaft-
    pflicht in der chemischen Industrie (1981);
    Schmidt-Salzer, BB 1983, 1251.

35  See eg BGHZ 29, 67; 45, 307; 69, 139; Mertens,
    op cit n. 21, 823 note 484.

36  See Bundesgerichtshof, Juristenzeitung 1983,
    497; Hager, AcP 84 (1984) 422.

37  See also BGHZ 80, 201; 86, 256; Bundes-
    gerichtshof, BB 1984, 2149; Diederichsen, Ver-
    sicherungsrecht 1984, Kallmann, BB 1985, 411.
    However, whether the distinction between the
    interest in "using" a certain product, typical,
    according to the court, of a contractual rela-
    tionship of and the interest in preserving the
    physical or property integrity, characteristic
    for delictual obligations, (BGHZ 86, 258)
    really helps, is, to put it mildly, doubtful.

38  Quite rightly Fleming, 4 Oxford Journal of
    Legal Studies 243, remarks therefore, "the
    culture flow is nowadays in reverse gear: to,
    not from, Europe; with European (and English)
    courts increasingly taking advantage of
    American experience especially in the new
    frontier areas of torts". As long as the
    courts react to specific experiences of a
    highly industrialized economy and society, the
    incentives necessarily come from wherever
    technological and economic development first
    leads to these experiences. At the same time,
    however, the "denationalization" of legal
    phenomena becomes more and more obvious.

39  See Priest, 56 Southern Cal L Rev 123 (1982).

40  Wasserhaushaltsgesetz Art 22; see also Kotz, AcP
    170 (1970) 36; Simitis, in Festschrift fur Duden
    628; Esser/Weyers, see n. 20.

41  See Fleming, 23 Am J Comp L 735 (1975); Taschner
    in: Zum deutschen internationalen Schuldrecht
    (1983), 75.

## PRODUCTS LIABILITY IN SWEDISH LAW

*Jan Hellner*


It would be nice to present Sweden as a country
which, in spite of its smallness, has solved the problems of products liability successfully. We should
then be able to offer to the world at large a survey
of our experience, letting the wise profit from our
achievement. Unfortunately, this is not the case.
Like many others, we are groping hesitantly with a
number of problems. The evolution has led into blind
alleys, and the confusion is perhaps greater now than
it was a few years ago. However, there might be
something to be learned from the way in which Sweden
has handled the problems.

## 1.   Case Law

When the Swedish Sale of Goods Act - which is based
on Scandinavian cooperation in legislation - was
enacted in 1905, it was realized that a problem
existed relating to products liability. This was
whether the rules concerning liability for defects in
goods sold should apply also to injuries to person
and to damage to property belonging to the buyer.
The case that was foremost in mind was that - known
already to Roman lawyers - in which cattle infected
with a contagious disease when sold and delivered to
a buyer transferred the disease to cattle already
belonging to the buyer. The application of the rules
relating to defects in goods would lead to somewhat
peculiar results under the Swedish Sale of Goods Act,
since liability to pay damages depends on whether the
goods were of a specific or a generic character. For
specific goods there is liability only for negligence
or for a guarantee (section 42, para 2), whereas for
generic goods the liability is strict, with an exception for *force majeure* (section 43, para 2). This
distinction - dubious in many situations - seems sin-
gularly unsuited to products liability. It was

stated in the *travaux préparatoires* – to which great
importance is attributed in Swedish law – that the
rules regarding liability for defects were not intended to apply to injury or damage caused by defective goods.[1] Such injury or damage should be judged
according to the law of tort.

The issue was presented squarely to the Supreme
Court of Sweden in 1918,[2] when a buyer claimed
damages because his cattle had been injured by
poisonous food supplied by a seller, without any
negligence being alleged on the part of the seller.
The Court decided that the rules of the Sale of Goods
Act did not apply, and no damages were awarded.
Since then, the main principle has been that a seller
is liable only for negligence and for failure to
conform to a guarantee. The care required by a
seller has been the subject of a number of decisions.
A seller was for instance considered to have a duty
to examine a second-hand bicycle with regard to the
safety that it offered to the user, before reselling
it. But as it was found that the defect which led to
an accident could not have been discovered at the
examination, the seller was not held liable.[3]

The leading case from 1918 concerns the liability of a seller, and it was therefore somewhat
uncertain whether the same principle should be
applied to a producer who was not himself a seller.
A case arose in which a woman who was making up a
bed-sofa was injured when a spring became loose and
hit her eye. It was found that the method of fasten-
ing the spring was dangerous, and the manufacturer
was held liable.[4] The lack of contractual privity
between the manufacturer and the woman does not even
seem to have attracted attention; it was obvious both
that the manufacturer must be ultimately responsible
for the construction of the bed-sofa and that the
seller would not examine the construction. It was
thus established that the principle of liability for
negligence applies also to a manufacturer.

As mentioned before, the rules of the Sale of
Goods Act do not apply to products liability. However, there are borderline cases, and they have
proved to be troublesome. One such case concerned
the fabrication of a compound to be used for the making of a dish consisting mainly of minced meat (the
case is known by the name of the dish, *"farsmacka"*,
apparently an adaptation of the German word
*"Vorschmack"*).[5] A millstone had broken when bread

---

* For footnotes see p. 140

was being ground and fragments of the stone mingled
with the crushed bread which was sold to the
manufacturer of the compound. As a result the whole
mixture was spoiled, and the manufacturer sued the
supplier of the crushed bread for damages for loss of
profit. The court when awarding damages stated
expressly that the Sale of Goods Act applied, and the
liability was strict. Since then, it is generally
admitted that for so-called "ingredient cases" the
rules of the Sale of Goods Act apply, and as the
ingredients are almost always generic goods the liability is strict. However, it is uncertain how far
the principle applies. That goods supplied by a
sub-manufacturer spoil the whole final product is
apparently common. According to insurers, damage of
this type causes them difficult problems, but they
have so far managed to settle the claims without
going to court.

Another problem concerns the role of a guarantee, especially if it is implied rather than express.
In one such case a farmer had ordered from a supplier
a substance suitable for destroying weeds in a
cultivation of the herb dill. The substance was
effective but unfortunately killed off the dill as
well. The supplier was held liable, and the Court
stated that the contract must be understood to imply
that the cultivation of dill would not be damaged by
the use of the weedkiller. [6] One may ask if a
similar reason could not be given in many other cases
in which goods sold cause damage or injury to the
buyer.

A couple of cases decided in 1977 seemed to
indicate that the Supreme Court was on its way to
introducing strict liability. In one of these cases,
a woman had bought hair-curlers and used them for
curling her hair. [7] The curlers got hot, and when she
cried out her son came to her assistance. The
curlers exploded and hot wax was thrown onto his
face. The curlers had been manufactured in Denmark
and a claim was brought against the importer, a
Swedish firm. The Supreme Court stated that the
curlers, because of their construction, presented a
considerable risk of such accidents as the one that
occurred to the son. It was not justifiable to put
such defective products onto the market, especially
as they were to be used by private persons without
any knowledge of technical questions. The manufacturer was therefore, although he was not a party
to the lawsuit, stated to be responsible for the
damage. The importer was then, in view of the fact
that the product was intended for private use, held
liable for injuries due to such unsafe products for

which the manufacturer was responsible. Clearly, in this case the Court was not far from holding the importer strictly liable for injuries caused by defective goods. It may be remarked that, although the Council of Europe Convention will impose liability on an importer, there is no other known case in Sweden, either earlier or later, in which an importer has been held liable without his own negligence, for injury or damage resulting from dangerous products.

In another case, decided in the same year, the manufacturer of a machine was held liable for an injury caused to a worker using the machine.[8] An accident similar to the one that caused the injury had occurred before, but this fact had not caused the responsible authorities to change the safety requirements relating to this type of machine. The conclusion is that a known risk, which is not suffi- cient to make the authorities change the safety requirements, may still be sufficient to make a manufacturer liable for negligence.

The Supreme Court of Sweden faced the issue of introducing strict liability in two cases which were decided comparatively recently. In both of these, the lower Courts had imposed strict liability, and the defendants appealed. In one of the cases the defendant had supplied food for hens, but the food was bad and the eggs acquired a taste that prevented them from being sold.[9] The Court stated that in view of the fact that legislation in the field of products liability was being contemplated (of which more presently), it was not willing to introduce strict liability which might come into conflict with the principles that were later to be enacted by the legislator. This statement was repeated in a somewhat later case, in which a horse had been poisoned by food supplied by the defendant.[10] In this case the effect of a guarantee was also considered. The horse was in the care of a trainer, who trained him for a race, and the trainer was the buyer of the food, whereas the plaintiff was the owner of the horse. The Court stated that since there was no direct contractual relation between the seller and the plaintiff, a guarantee could not put the plaintiff in a more favourable position than he would be under general principles of liability.

It might be observed that the two earlier cases concerned injury to persons, whereas the two latter ones concerned damage to property, although of a kind that is sometimes alleged to justify exceptional liability, i.e. injuries to domestic animals caused by defective food.

Another recent case turned mainly on the problem of causation.[11]    Some patients who had undergone X-ray examination of the spine suffered paralysation injuries, and an action was brought against the manufacturer of the contrast fluid which had been used. The injection of the fluid was so painful that it had to be combined with the use of a local anaesthetic.   There were two issues in the case, one whether there was any negligence by the manufacturer of the contrast fluid, and the other whether there was any causal connection between the use of the contrast fluid and the injury.  The majority of the Court decided that it was so uncertain whether the contrast fluid - rather than the anaesthetic - was the cause of the injury, that a causal connection could not be considered to be sufficiently proved. The minority of the Court also came to the conclusion that the manufacturer of the fluid was not liable, but although they found that a causal connection had been proved there was, in their opinion, no proved negligence.   By way of comment on the view of the majority regarding the causation, it might be added that if a suit had been brought against the manufacturer of the anaesthetic, it seems probable that the outcome would have been the same. It would have been argued that it was so uncertain that the anaesthetic rather than the contrast fluid was the cause, that liability could not be imposed on this manufacturer either.   (The possibility that the injury was caused by the combination of the contrast fluid and the anaesthetic was ruled out on the basis of the extensive scientific evidence that was presented in the case.)

The wave towards imposing strict liability by case law has apparently ebbed. The principal reason given - that legislation is being contemplated - may seen insufficient to some observers, especially since it does not seem likely that all-embracing legislation will be enacted within the foreseeable future.

## 2.   Preparations for Legislation

In 1973 a government commission started work on pre-paring legislation on products liability. The first report of the commission concerned injuries to person caused by drugs.[12]   The commission proposed the institution of a compulsory insurance, to be taken out by manufacturers and importers of drugs. The proposal was not carried into effect, but it was a dominant factor in the introduction of a voluntary insurance of which more will be said presently.

The commission then proceeded to propose a general statute on products liability, based on the Council of Europe Convention of 1977.[13] In conformity with the Convention, the general principle was to be one of strict liability for injuries to persons caused by defective goods. However, the proposal did not conform entirely to the Convention but contained some original features. It was realized at the time when the commission's proposal was published that the Convention would never enter into force in its present shape, as it would have to conform to the EC directive when such a directive was passed. However, in the opinion of the commission, the main principles of the Council of Europe Convention were acceptable to Sweden, and the proposed legislation should prepare the ground for a future adhesion to the Convention. The proposal had a mixed reception. Consumer organizations were generally in favour of it, whereas both the manufacturing industry and the insurers were against it. Strict liability was not congenial to industry, and it was pointed out that there was no great advantage in enacting a statute before it was known what a Convention would contain. No legislation based on the proposal has been enacted.

As for damage to goods - which was not included in the proposal for legislation based on the Council of Europe Convention - two proposals have appeared recently. One is contained in a draft Consumer Services Act, on which work has proceeded so far that a bill to the Swedish Riksdag was expected in the autumn of 1984.[14] This draft Act contains rules on liability for defects in services, and the rules are to apply also to damage caused to the property of the consumer and his family. The liability is to be based on a presumption of fault, i.e. the enterprise must, if it is to escape liability, prove that the damage was not caused by its negligence or the negligence of someone for whom it is responsible. Since the Act is to apply only to services rendered by an enterprise to a consumer - mainly to repair of houses, cars, boats and consumer goods in general - the importance of the proposed rule is limited. In addition, in a recent report on a revised Consumer Sales Act, it is proposed that the rules relating to liability for defects in goods sold shall apply to damage to property belonging to the buyer or a member of his household and which is intended for personal use.[15] This liability is to be strict, with exception for *force majeure*. Since this proposal was published in May 1984, its future is at present

uncertain. It is possible that the rules relating to
services rendered to consumers and goods delivered to
consumers will be adjusted to each other; anyhow it
seems curious to an outsider that they should be
different. Another questions which might be raised,
a *propos* of the two proposals, is what rules should
apply when, e.g., goods are rented by a consumer.
Leases of cars are, for instance, common. Altogether,
the future seems uncertain in this field too.

## 3. Insurance

The most important Swedish contribution to solving
the problems of products liability is undoubtedly the
institution of the "pharmaceutical injuries insurance", which was introduced in 1978.[16] As mentioned
before, a commission had proposed a compulsory
insurance, but instead this voluntary insurance was
created. Manufacturers of drugs, insurers and others
(including representatives of the Ministry of
Justice) cooperated in elaborating the conditions.
The basis of the insurance is found in an undertaking
by manufacturers and importers of drugs to compensate
those suffering injuries from drugs on a level which
corresponds to that of tort damages. This
undertaking is covered by a collective insurance
administered by a group of insurers. Adhesion to
the insurance is voluntary, but all Swedish
manufacturers adhered from the beginning, and the
importers have done so to an increasing extent. At
present practically all suppliers of drugs partici-
pate.

The main question is to decide which injuries
from drugs are to be covered. The rules are fairly
complicated. The liability is not based on either
negligence or defects. The main object is to cover
those severe losses that cannot be considered to be
the probable consequences of the illness which caused
the use of the drug. If a severe illness necessi-
tates the use of a drug, which is known to have
adverse side effects, the emergence of these effects
does not entitle the sufferer to compensation. On
the other hand, if a drug taken because of a slight
illness unexpectedly leads to a severe complication,
compensation is awarded. An example may be
mentioned. Sulfa drugs are commonly administered in
modern medical practice, and for some illnesses they
are routine and almost necessary treatment. A very
few of those who are treated with sulfa drugs develop
what is called Lyell's syndrome, a terrible disease
characterized by wounds in the face and elsewhere.
On the basis of liability for negligence, the victims
would not be compensated, as there are good grounds

for administering the drug and apparently there is no
way to predict whether the syndrome will appear or
not. Nor can the syndrome be ascribed to any defect in
the drug, at least not present in the state of knowledge.

It might be argued that one should hold a doctor
or a hospital liable if the drug is administered without informing the patient of the risk.
In my opinion this argument does not hold. If the
risk is very slight, the patient will normally take
it, and the fact that he knowingly did so should not
deprive him of the right of compensation. On the
other hand, in the case of a severe illness, with-
holding information should not be a sufficient ground
for granting compensation for personal injury,
supposing that there was no doubt that the treatment
was necessary. This opinion does not concern the
question whether information should be given or not,
only the issue whether the right to compensation for
personal injury should depend on lack of information.

As just mentioned, the conditions are rather
complicated, and the decision whether compensation is
awarded is often taken on a test of reasonableness,
which of course may lead to considerable doubt.
There is a ceiling of SEK 2 millions for each injured
person and another ceiling of SEK 150 millions for
injuries occurring during each calendar year. There
must be a preponderance of probability that the
injury has been caused by the drug. Some provisions
aim at reducing administration costs as far as
possible. Slight injuries are not covered. In
practice, claims for compensation are refused to a
considerable extent. If the claimant is not satisfied with the decision of the insurers, he can bring
the matter to a special board, consisting of eight
members, some of them impartial, others representing
interested organizations. If the claimant is not
content with the decision of the board, the matter
may be brought to arbitrators.

The pharmaceutical injuries insurance is one instance of the voluntary "no-fault" insurance that is
found in Sweden at present.[17] The others are the
"security insurance for work-connected injuries" and
the "patient insurance". It is typical of this kind
of insurance that it is based on an agreement between
the parties interested that tort liability is replaced by insurance in favour of those suffering
injuries, that the right to compensation does not
depend on either negligence or a defect, and that the
conditions in general aim at reducing administration
costs as far as possible. For both the patient
insurance and the pharmaceutical injuries insurance a

principal aim is to cover the unexpected injuries
that, in view of the circumstances, may be considered
unforeseeable accidents. In addition the insurance
covers a great number of injuries that would be
covered under general rules of tort or contract
liability. But neither insurance covers each and
every complication that arises from medical
treatment. The ideas are insurance ideas rather than
tort ideas. The principal initiator of this type of
insurance is a legal officer of the Skandia insurance
company, Mr Carl Oldertz.

There is no compulsion for a person suffering an
injury from a drug to turn to pharmaceutical injuries
insurance rather than to sue for damages in tort.
But as the possibilities of receiving compensation
are better under the conditions of the insurance
scheme, tort claims for injuries from drugs are now
rare. There have been a number of tort claims for
deaths allegedly caused by contraceptive pills, but
no causal connection has been proved so far in these
cases.

Liability insurance covering tort liability has
been available for a long time in Sweden, but it
seems somewhat dubious to me whether its operation
can be considered successful so far. At first the
general liability insurance of enterprises covered
products liability based on tort. Then a special
products liability insurance was introduced, and the
conditions of the general enterprise liability
insurance were adjusted in order to exclude products
liability in general. Only so much remained as to
suit the requirements of those enterprises that considered the risk of incurring products liability so
slight that they would not contemplate procuring a
special insurance.

The conditions of the products liability insurance have presented some difficulties for the Swedish
insurers. In the first place, the conditions contain
some exceptions which, if applied literally, might
exclude insurance protection even in situations where
it would be considered needed and justified, at least
in the opinion of the insured. In the second place,
the general exception for liability undertaken by
contract, in excess of liability emerging from
general principles of law, has been found to be
unsuitable. Some standard form contracts in common
use impose strict liability up to limited amounts in
situations for which general rules only impose
liability for negligence. Accordingly, an insured
using such a standard form contract might find his
liability excluded from the insurance coverage. The

conditions have been adjusted in order to comply
with this requirement of the insured. However, it
is exceptional for standard form contracts to
impose stricter liability than general rules do. It
is much more common for them to contain exemption
clauses, and these also create problems. Normally,
an insurer will be allowed to avail himself of an
exemption clause in his client's contract as a
defence. But the client might be unwilling to
invoke a far-reaching exemption clause, which was
intended mostly for cases in which there was no
liability insurance. The Swedish insurers have
resorted to various devices to deal with this
problem but there is no consensus among them on
what is the best solution.

A major insurer has returned to the practice of
including products liability coverage in the general
liability insurance of enterprises, as part of an
extension of the scope of this insurance. In this
way, contractual liability is included to a considerable extent. This apparent generosity is diminished
by other clauses, which diminish the insurer's liability. The other Swedish insurers do not seem
inclined to follow suit, and the general situation
appears somewhat unclear.

4.    General Reflections

Products liability is much discussed in Sweden, as in
many other countries, but its practical importance
seems to be smaller than one would gather from the
discussion. We should distinguish between various
types of injury and damage.

The discussion on products liability is often
concentrated on injuries to persons. The Council of
Europe Convention is limited to such injuries. For
Sweden, injuries to persons play a limited role.
Social insurance covers the dominant part of the
losses that arise, and as there is no subrogation
from social insurance towards a tortfeasor, these
losses remain on the social insurance. The prepond-
erant part of tort damages (and of insurance compensation assessed on the same principles as tort
damages) at present goes to the compensation of pain
and suffering and similar losses, in spite of the
fact that such compensation is comparatively low in
Sweden.

Some of the losses that might otherwise be important are now covered by "no-fault" insurance which
leaves little or no room for products liability. A
case was mentioned previously (p.130, n.8) in which a

worker had been injured by a machine which was unsafe. Such a case would hardly come before the
Swedish courts at present, since there is a so-called
"security insurance for work-connected injuries".
Under the conditions of this insurance, the worker
would be entitled to compensation on the tort level,
without regard to any negligence by his employer, a
manufacturer or anyone else. Products liability is
thus eliminated for industrial accidents whenever the
injury is covered by the "security insurance". This
insurance is based on a collective agreement between
employers and trade unions. Even if the individual
employer omits to take out insurance, the employee is
protected. If the employees are covered, the
insurance also applies to the employer in his work.
The self-employed, such as farmers, have procured the
same kind of protection through their organisations.
The great majority of the working force are thus
protected. However, there is a small minority who
are not covered by the "security insurance", and for
them tort liability, including products liability,
remains the means for covering the part of the loss
that exceeds social insurance.

For motor traffic accidents, liability has even
smaller importance. There is a compulsory insurance
operating in favour of all victims of motor traffic,
including the drivers, and the victims of such accidents will turn to it for compensation. In accordance with the general policy of excluding subrogation
claims as far as possible, the traffic insurer has
recourse towards a tortfeasor only in very exceptional cases. A subrogation claim based on products
liability would succeed only if the defendant had
been guilty of intentional misconduct or gross negligence, an extremely unlikely case.

The situation with regard to injuries from drugs
has been described already. The case of the contrast
fluid (p. 131, n.11) occurred before the
pharmaceutical injuries insurance was in force, and
at present it would probably have been handled under
the conditions of this insurance. Whether the question of causation would have been decided differently
from what the majority of the Supreme Court concluded
is very difficult to say. The basis on which the
minority of the Court dismissed the claim, i.e. that
there was no negligence, would have been irrelevant
under the conditions of the pharmaceutical injuries
insurance, and the exceptions in the conditions of
this insurance would in all probability not have
applied. The possibility of receiving compensation
from the pharmaceutical injuries insurance does not
preclude a party from suing in court on a tort basis,

but, as mentioned before, such suits are exceptional. The fact that it is often extremely difficult to prove or to disprove a causal link between the use of a drug and an injury will apparently continue to create a problem, whatever system is employed, and it is not easy to see how it can be solved.

The case of the hair curlers (p. 129, n.7) illustrates the problems arising from the use of cosmetics and other products by private persons in their homes. It seems likely that such injuries will remain the principal field of products liability for personal injuries in Sweden in the future.

Whereas Swedish enterprises seem to regard products liability for personal injuries occurring in Sweden with some tranquillity, this is not the case with injuries that are caused by Swedish products in other countries. Where social insurance is not so highly developed, or where it is combined with a right of subrogation towards tortfeasors, the damages that are to be paid may be very high. Indeed, one of the objections raised by the Swedish industry against the introduction of strict products liability on an international level was that, whereas foreign enterprises selling their products in Sweden and causing injuries there would profit from the high level of social insurance, a Swedish manufacturer causing an injury in a foreign country would have to pay damages on a much higher level. The argument may not be decisive from a logical or an economic point of view, but its psychological impact might be understood.

According to Swedish insurers, products liability for damage to property is more important than for personal injuries. The "ingredient cases" and other damage on the border between damage to property and pure economic loss create problems. The cases relating to food for animals mentioned above may illustrate the problem of distinguishing between liability for negligence and strict liability, but the type of damage that they exemplify is not of great economic importance. Damage resulting from defective ingredients or from defective goods that become components of machines and spoil both the machine and raw material causes much greater problems, especially as it is often uncertain on whom, in a long chain of manufacturers, distributors and retailers, the liability should fall.

Neither Sweden case law nor Swedish insurance conditions seem to have reached satisfactory solutions of these problems. Talks with Swedish insurance companies have given me the impression that claims are often handled on a non-legal, common sense basis. The insurers try to form a judgement whether the damage or loss that has arisen should be treated as the kind of accident that should be covered by insurance, or as the manifestation of a business risk arising from a defective performance which should be borne by the client himself. Damage arising from a more or less excusable mistake in providing one product when the intention was to provide another belong to the first category, for which insurance coverage is supposed to be justified. The foreseeable consequences of providing goods of an unsatisfactory quality belong to the second category. There are a number of intermediary situations for which the judgement is more or less intuitive. When the insurer has formed his opinion, he will have to persuade his client that it is correct and justified, and anyhow he has to try to reach an agreement with him. Whether it is easier for the insurer to reach an agreement with his client when relying on the commonsense arguments rather than the niceties of legal principles is unknown to me.

There are of course a great number of problems that have not presented themselves to either courts or legislators in Sweden. One that has already been mentioned in passing concerns the placing of the liability when goods have passed through several hands and it is uncertain on whom the responsibility for a defect is to rest. Another question concerns the handling of the responsibility when several factors have contributed causally to the injury or damage. The omission of any discussion of such problems does not mean that I do not realize their importance, only that Sweden has no experience in dealing with them.

As indicated before, the only claim that Sweden can make to having contributed to the solution of the problems of products liability is by the institution of the "pharmaceutical products insurance". The principles that appear in the conditions of this insurance were characterized as being based on insurance ideas rather than tort ideas. The same is true of other types of "no-fault" insurance, particularly the patient insurance. In my opinion, these ideas deserve serious discussion, but it would carry us far beyond the precincts of products liability.

## 5. The Impact of the EEC Directive

Although Sweden is not a member of the EEC, the publication of the EEC Directive on products liability has changed the situation in Sweden entirely. Steps are being taken for the preparation of new legislation. It is not likely that a new commission for preparing legislation will be set up, but work will be carried out in the Department of Justice. It is not known what the new proposals will mean; only some general observations can be made.

It is expected that the Council of Europe Convention will be amended, in such a way that it will be possible for Member States of the EEC to ratify it. A consequence will be that the states that are not members of the EEC but wish to be able to ratify the Council of Europe Convention will be affected indirectly. However, there might be one important difference from what will be the case in states belonging to the EEC. The Directive is binding in both directions. Not only must every Member State introduce legislation that fulfils the requirements of the Directive; it must not introduce new legislation imposing stricter liability on producers than the Directive prescribes, with certain exceptions, principally for development risks and for agricultural products. It appears to be unlikely that the same will be true for the Council of Europe Convention. In consequence, it would be possible for a country like Sweden, which wishes to ratify the Council of Europe Convention but is not bound by the Directive, to impose stricter liability on producers than the EEC Directive permits. It is impossible to predict whether or to what extent Sweden will take advantage of this greater liberty of action.

## FOOTNOTES

1      Nytt Juridiskt Arkiv II 1906 No. 1 p 80.

2      Nytt Juridiskt Arkiv I 1981, p 156. (It is customary in Sweden to identify Supreme Court decisions solely by reference to the page in the official reports in which they appear.)

3      Nytt Juridiskt Arkiv 1944, p 83.

4      Nytt Juridiskt Arkiv 1961, p 94.

5      Nytt Juridiskt Arkiv 1960, p 441.

6      Nytt Juridiskt Arkiv 1968, p 285.

7      Nytt Juridiskt Arkiv 1977, p 538.

8      Nytt Juridiskt Arkiv 1977, p 788.

9      Nytt Juridiskt Arkiv 1982, p 380.

10    Nytt Juridiskt Arkiv 1983, p 118.

11    Nytt Juridiskt Arkiv 1982, p 421.

12    Produktansvar  I.  Ersattning  for  lakemedels-
      skada. Statens Offentliga Utredningar 1976:23.

13    See  Produktansvar  II.  Produktansvarslag.
      Statens Offentliga Utredningar 1979:79.

14    The  proposal  was  submitted  to  the  so-called
      Council of Law in May 1984. The  relevant  pro-
      vision  is section 31, para  2.  (Konsumenttjan-
      stlag 1985:716).

15    See  Ny  Konsumentkoplag.  Statens  Offentliga
      Utredningar 1984:25, section 27.

16    The present conditions have been in force  since
      1   January 1981.  See C Olderetz, Patient-  och
      Lakemedelssakadeforsakringarna,        Tidskrift
      utgiven  av  Juridiska  Foreningen  i  Finland,
      1981, pp 378 ff.

17    See  in  general  J  Hellner,  Haftungsersetzung
      durch  Versicherungsschutz  in  Schweden,  in
      Fleming/Hellner/von   Hippel,  Haftungsersetzung
      durch Versicherungsschutz, Arbeiten zur Rechts-
      vergleichung Frankfurt am Main 1980, pp 24 ff.

## THE STATUS OF PRODUCTS LIABILITY LAW IN THE UNITED STATES OF AMERICA

*Jerry J. Phillips*

### 1.  Strict Liability

The battle rages stateside over the proper scope of strict liability in the sale of products. It seems fairly well settled that strict liability applies in the case of the sale of a product containing a so-called manufacturing or production flaw - that is, one that departs from the norm.[1] However, even here only a standard of due care is imposed if the product can be categorized as "unavoidably unsafe".[2] Probably comment (k) of the Second Restatement of Torts,[3] from which the unavoidably unsafe rationale is derived, contemplated only the inclusion of drugs within this category, but the cases have reflected no such limitation.[4] There is no agreement as to what kinds of products are properly describable as unavoidably unsafe.

Nor can the production flaw be readily distinguished from the design flaw. A design feature is supposedly characteristic of an entire line of products; but a method of production or formulation - which surely is a design - may in fact result only in random defects.[5] Conversely, an entire run may contain "production" defects because of an inadvertent omission or commission in the production process. It is sometimes said that a design feature results from a conscious choice;[6] but then, so may a method of testing which can result in production flaws.[7]

It is widely, although not universally, stated that - at least for manufacturers - liability for

---

*    For footnotes see p.153

design and warning defects is measured only by a
standard of due care.[8] In the case of design, this
approach is explainable by the fact that the defect
is usually judged by a balancing standard of the risk
of danger versus the burden of prevention.[9]
Concretely, application of this standard means the
plaintiff must show that the product can be
redesigned so as to prevent the present substantial
danger, and that this can be done without creating
other equally serious dangers, destroying the product's utility, or rendering it cost-prohibitive.
Since the manufacturer is held to the standard of an
expert,[10] failure to make such a practical redesign
would constitute a lack of due care. In California,
the defendant has the burden of showing that such a
redesign is not practicable.[11]

There is an indication in some of the decisions
that a product can be defective, or unreasonably dangerous, in design because of failure to meet ordinary
consumer expectations, without regard to whether a
safer redesign is practicable.[12] It is also
recognized, at least in dictum, that some products
may be so unsafe that they should not be marketed at
all - again, without regard to the practicability of
redesign.[13]

Where failure to warn, or inadequate warning, is
alleged, the courts tend to think in terms of a due
care standard[14] because of the difficulty of con-
ceiving of warning about a danger which is unknown
and unknowable. Of course this conceptual difficulty
is no different for the production defect, where true
strict liability is typically imposed. Also, in
exploring the practicalities of giving an effective
warning the courts tend to think in due care
terms.[15]

An area in which American courts widely impose
true strict liability is for breach of express warranty or misrepresentation.[16] Here it is immaterial
whether the warranty or representation was capable of
being performed, as long as the plaintiff relied on
the false representation to his or her detriment. It
is not clear to what extent reliance must be shown,
or whether reliance, if necessary, must be by the
plaintiff or can be by someone else.[17]

The United States Supreme Court has held that
the free speech and press clauses of the first amendment to the United States Constitution prohibit the
imposition of strict liability for defamation; some
fault must be shown - knowing or reckless falsity in
the case of a public plaintiff, and lack of due care

in the case of a private plaintiff.[18]  It is possible
that  these rules apply only to media defendants, and
to defendants using the media,[19] although there is no
agreement as to the definition of the media.[20]  It is
unclear  whether  these  rules might apply to product
misrepresentation,[21]  although  some  courts  using
defamation  decisions  as  precedents have refused to
impose strict liability for product disparagement.[22]

    A  final  pocket  of strict liability that may be
applicable  to products suppliers is that imposed for
ultrahazardous  or  abnormally  dangerous  activities.
The Americans acquired this doctrine from the British
via  *Rylands v Fletcher.*[23]  The reach of the doctrine
is  unknown,  in  large  part because  there  is  no
agreement  as  to  its essential operative feature or
features.[24]     The   abnormally-dangerous-activity
doctrine does not require proof of a defect, however,
as  that  term  is  typically  used  in  traditional
products liability, so application of the doctrine to
the  supply of products has far-reaching implications
in this regard.

2.    Privity - Economic Loss

The  requirement  of  privity in the case of physical
injuries  has  gone  by  the  board in negligence and
strict  tort, and largely also in implied warranty.[25]
The physically injured plaintiff need not be a buyer,
user  or  consumer  of the product.  He may be a mere
bystander.[26]   The  only  requirement  is that he be
foreseeable,  and  foreseeability  is construed quite
broadly for this purpose.[27]

    When  the plaintiff has suffered solely economic
loss,  however, as opposed to physical injury to person  or property, then the decisions are in disarray.
The  alleged  majority position is that the plaintiff
suffering only economic loss (e.g. decrease in market
value  of  the  product,  or  lost  profits) must sue
either  in  express warranty, with or without privity
of  contract, or in implied warranty and then only if
there  is  privity  between  the  plaintiff  and
defendant.[28]  There is no agreement as to what constitutes  physical harm,  or whether the concept includes
harm  to  the product itself.[29]  Probably most of the
cases  would  define  physical  harm  as  a  sudden
traumatic injury caused by the defective product, and
would  include damage solely to the product itself.[30]
However,  it  is  clear that one can also sue in tort
without  privity  for  a  gradually accruing personal
injury,  such as asbestosis.[31]  Apparently all of the
cases  agree  that if there is physical harm, however
defined,  then any foreseeable economic loss suffered

is recoverable also.[32]

The reasons usually given for the solely-econo-mic-loss rules are that they are necessary so the seller will not be held liable for the peculiar needs of the buyer, and so the seller can disclaim or limit liability.[33] It has been pointed out, however, that not all (or even most) economic losses are freakish or unforeseeable.[34] Moreover, whether a disclaimer or limited remedy should be upheld should turn on the status of the parties as equal bargainors, and not on the nature of the injury or the theory of recovery. When there is no privity, then the only way bargaining can be effected is by means of an intermediary such as a retailer who can deal directly with the buyer on behalf of the manufacturer.

It is possible that the concern over recovery for solely economic loss stems from the probably commercial uninsurability of such loss.[35] If this concern is the basis of the so-called majority position, then it is curious that it is never ex-pressed in the opinions. The widespread use of self-insurance, particularly among large manufac-turers, undercuts this concern. Moreover, perhaps the question should be not whether such loss is cur-rently insurable commercially, but whether commercial insurers should be required to provide such insurance coverage.

### 3.  The Non-Manufacturing Seller

There has been a growing concern about holding the non-manufacturing seller strictly liable when the manufacturer can also be held liable. Such dual liability is viewed as redundant and economically wasteful. Accordingly, the proposed federal Products Liability Act and several state laws release the non-manufacturing seller from strict liability unless he holds himself out as the manufacturer or expressly warrants the goods, or unless the manufacturer is insolvent or not subject to service of process.[36]

It seems a bit odd to condition one's liability on whether or not another is subject to service of process. Be that as it may, such laws are likely to breed more confusion and litigation than certainty and cost savings. Representations (express warranties), in the form of advertisements and other-wise, permeate the modern law of American products liability,[37] and removal of implied liability for the non-manufacturing seller would impose substantial pressures toward the expansion of representational liability. Moreover, it may be difficult to determine at the time suit is filed whether a defendant is in fact subject to service or is insolvent.[38]    In addition, a defendant may become insolvent during the course of litigation. What is the plaintiff to do in these situations, guess at his peril?

4.    Mass Tort Litigation

A salient feature of American products litigation that has become prominent in the last quarter of the twentieth century is mass tort litigation, characterized by the hundreds and thousands of suits precipitated by such products as asbestos, diethylstilboestrol (DES), and Agent Orange. It is likely that such litigation will become much more prevalent in the next few decades, as the vast dangers from carcinogens and toxic wastes become more apparent.[39] A number of people are beginning to question whether the common law system of tort litigation is capable of handling such massive disputes.[40] The recent bankruptcy of the Manville Corporation has highlighted the problem.[41]

There are a number of special features that are associated with mass tort litigation. One is the inability of the plaintiff to identify the causal defendant - a problem especially present in the DES litigation since the drug was sold generically.[42] The courts' responses to this problem have been varied - all the way from denying liability because of failure of proof of causation,[43] to imposing several liability based on percentage of market share,[44] to imposing joint liability on all sued defendants based on concert of action[45] or risk contribution.[46] Where, on the other hand, the plaintiff can show that a defendant has tortiously contributed in part to his injury, but cannot show the extent of such contribution, the plaintiff typically is allowed a joint and several judgment for all damages against such defendant under well-accepted tort principles.[47]

Injuries or diseases that develop over a long period of time present special problems with regard to recoverable damages and insurability. In the asbestos cases, plaintiffs who have been diagnosed as having asbestos are fearful that their ailment may later turn into a cancer such as mesothelioma, and they seek to recover damages for this fear and for the medical costs and suffering involved in monitoring their condition.[48] Recovery of such damages is fairly well accepted.[48]

A much more difficult problem arises where the plaintiff has not yet contracted any disease, but fears that he or she may, and wishes to recover for fear and for pain and costs involved in medical monitoring. This is the case with daughters of mothers who ingested DES during pregnancy. Certainly the medical costs are tangible and quantifiable, but the fear may be speculative or at least not statistically supportable. Also, such claims present difficult problems of res judicata and splitting of the cause of action, should the plaintiff later actually develop cancer. Massachusetts has allowed such fear claims where the plaintiffs have developed some physical injury from the drug, but has denied the claim where there is no demonstrable physical injury.[49] It would seem, however, that the costs of medical monitoring would qualify as physical injury for this purpose.

The insurability questions for slowly maturing diseases are particularly complex. The typical American products liability insurance policy provides for indemnity of the insured for products claims arising out of an "occurrence" resulting in bodily injury.[50] The "occurrence" may be viewed as the time of exposure or of multiple exposures, the time of maturation of the disease, or the time of manifestation. Different courts have held that each of the times is the operative event[51] and at least one court has held that all of these times are operative, making all insurers over the entire relevant time period jointly and severally liable.[52] Asbestos insurers have filed a number of law suits contesting their liability, and it has been suggested that the insurers' recalcitrance against paying claims was the decisive factor in forcing Manville into bankruptcy.[53]

The Fifth Circuit has held as a matter of law that no further punitive damages may be awarded in suits against asbestos manufacturers, because such awards are likely to deplete funds available for compensatory damage awards and because defendants have been punished enough.[54] The parties have the option in a punitive damage case to show the fact finder the extent of the defendant's wealth, and the defendant may also show the jury how much it has already been punished by punitive damage awards, in order to determine the appropriateness of further such awards.[55] Obviously, the defendant will be hard put to decide whether prior punitive awards should be revealed to the jury. The court also has broad discretion to reduce an excessive punitive award.[56] The action of the Fifth Circuit in barring all such

future awards in that court is, however, an
extraordinary holding and apparently one of first
impression.[57]

The fact that defendant has liability insurance
is not deemed legally relevant in determining the
wealth of the defendant,[58] although as a practical
matter of course it is very relevant and its availability greatly undermines the deterrent force of a
punitive award. A recommendation of the Insurance
Services Office that liability insurance should not
provide coverage for punitive damages was stoutly
resisted by the insurance industry, in main because
of the grave conflict of interest problems that would
arise if the insurer could defend on grounds of
non-coverage because of the presence of wilful or
reckless misconduct on the part of the insured.[59] A
few jurisdictions, however, hold that it is against
public policy to provide liability insurance coverage
for punitive damage awards.[60]

## 5.   Comparative Fault and Contribution

Within the past two decades there has been a substantial movement at the state level toward the adoption,
either judicially or by statute, of a system of
comparative fault. The majority of jurisdictions have
adopted, usually by statute, a partial comparative
fault system whereby the plaintiff can recover only
if his fault is less or not greater than that of the
defendant. A minority of states allows the plaintiff
to recover if the defendant is at fault in any
degree.[61]

Professor John Wade contends that the sudden
movement towards comparative fault sprang from a
desire to ameliorate one of the harshest features of
the common law of torts - namely, contributory negligence as a complete bar-in order to blunt the drive
for adoption of automobile no-fault plans in this
country.[62] Whatever the reason, the no-fault movement appears to have ground to a halt in America,
with the adoption of varying watered-down plans in
about fifteen states and no prospects of passage of
such a plan at the national level.[63]

In those states that have adopted a comparative
fault system, the overwhelming trend is to apply the
doctrine in strict products liability.[64] Insofar as
products liability is not really strict liability but
is in fact based on fault, application of the system
presents no doctrinal difficulty. But in the context
of true strict liability, use of comparative fault
remains in search of a doctrinal justification. A

causal analysis is hardly helpful, since both the
defendant's and the plaintiff's conduct must be a
substantial cause before the doctrine applies.

The overwhelming majority of jurisdictions that
have adopted comparative fault retain the doctrine of
joint and several liability, rather than several or
proportioned liability, where there is more than one
tortfeasor.[65] The basic policy justification for
doing this is that contributory negligence differs in
kind from primary negligence, since it is directed at
the plaintiff himself rather than others and is
therefore less culpable; the risk of loss, then, is
thought more properly to rest on the more culpable
party.[66]

For purposes of comparison in a partial comparative system, the plaintiff's fault may be compared
against each defendant individually or against all
defendants. Probably the latter method of comparison
is the more common.[67]

The sibling of comparative fault is contribution
among defendants. Curiously, all jurisdictions that
have comparative fault do not have contribution, and
vice versa. Even in those jurisdictions that have
both systems, the methods of comparison in each
system - e.g. pro rata or per capita - may vary.[68]

One of the most vexing areas of contribution has
to do with workplace capital goods injuries, typically the brake press injury where the machine is
alleged to lack adequate guards or other safety
devices. These injuries are responsible for something approaching one half of the products liability
payouts in America.[69] In many cases the employer may
be at fault, but is immune from contribution to the
machine manufacturer owing to the exclusive remedy
provisions of most American workers' compensation
schemes. To add insult to injury, in a number of
jurisdictions the culpable employer has a subrogation
lien against the machine manufacturer to recover any
workers' compensation benefits paid to the injured
worker.[70] Owing to the complicated interplay of
conflicting interests involved, this unhappy
situation remains largely unresolved.

6.   Successor Corporation Liability

Within the past decade there has been a tremendous
upsurge in the amount of products litigation in which
the plaintiff seeks to hold a successor corporation
liable for injuries caused by a defective product
sold by a predecessor corporation. The basis of this

doctrine is in the corporate law of de facto merger
or business enterprise continuity, wherein typically
there had to be an exchange of predecessor assets for
successor stock, with the predecessor dissolving
shortly after the exchange, and the successor
continuing the predecessor's business and product
line with a continuity of employees and
management.[71]

Under pressure of the developing law of products
liability, the courts have begun to depart from the
corporate criteria in determining successor
liability. Several leading decisions have dispensed
with the requirement that the exchange be for
stock;[72] a few courts have dispensed with the predecessor dissolution requirement;[73] and there is no
consensus on the requirement of management or
employee continuity.[74]

While the old corporate criteria have been
steadily eroded, there is no agreement on what the
emerging products liability criteria should be. Specifically, the question is: how much continuity is
necessary? Must the exact same product be sold? The
same name used? Is it enough if the same patents,
copyrights, logos, customer lists, employees, or
plant be used? So far, the cases have been
adjudicated essentially on an ad hoc basis.[75] Here,
as in so many areas of the developing law of American
products liability, the law is in a state of change
and in search of a consistent rationale.

7.   The Scope of Products Liability

The law of products liability is, across the board,
in a state of fluctuation, growth and change. The
courts daily wrestle with questions of the definition
of defectiveness,[76] the meaning of strict liability,[77] proof of causation,[78] and burdens of proof
in general.[79]

In addition, there is constant pressure to
expand the law of products liability, especially
strict liability, to new areas. The concept of the
product is itself being extended to intangibles,[80]
and to land.[81] Products law has been applied to
leases, bailments, licences,[82] and to the furnishing
of goods where no transfer of property interest is
contemplated.[83] There is an emerging trend to apply
strict products liability law to occupiers of
business premises.[84] The law is being extended to
testers, franchisers, licensers,[85] and it may well
soon include mere advertisers. Similarly, the
providers of professional services - doctors,

lawyers, architects, and the like – may be brought within the penumbras of products law.[86]

In 1914 Professor Jeremiah Smith wrote that the public "are not likely to be content for long" under the "two conflicting theories" of negligence law on the one hand, and strict but limited workers' compensation liability on the other.[87] Yet the two systems continue to exist side by side in America, albeit uneasily, seventy years later. So it is also with strict products liability and the more general tort law of negligence in America today. Undoubtedly there will be continued sparring for position between the two doctrines during the foreseeable future. It is unlikely that America will adopt a comprehensive administrative scheme of payment like that currently in effect in New Zealand,[88] if for no other reason because of the sheer size of the cost involved.[89] Rather, the fight is likely to be carried on in the common law courts and the legislatures between pro-plaintiff and pro-defendant interests, with the battle lines constantly shifting from time to time and place to place.

## 8.    Proposed Federal Legislation

For the last several years there have been massive efforts on the part of manufacturing and insurance interests to obtain codification of the law of products liability. Products statutes with widely varying provisions have been enacted at the state level in about thirty states,[90] but that movement appears to have ground to a halt. Now a gargantuan effort has been launched by the same interests to obtain passage of products legislation at the federal level.[91] Equally powerful consumer and attorney interests have been massed in opposition to the proposed legislation. The result is that Washington, D.C., is caught today in the throes of a major lobbying campaign on the issue of products legislation.

The presently proposed federal bill would abolish strict liability for design and failure to warn; it would significantly limit the scope of the duty to warn; it would generally relieve non-manufacturing sellers from products liability; it would adopt pure comparative fault, and abolish joint and several liability. It would immunize the plaintiff's employer from claims for contribution or indemnity. It would establish a statute of repose of uncertain scope, restrict recoverable punitive damages, substantially narrow the admissibility of post-accident remedial measures, probably require defendant identification in every case, and it would abolish recovery in products liability for economic loss or injury to the product itself.[92]

The alleged purpose of the bill is to achieve national uniformity in the area of products law.[93] It is unlikely, however, that the proposed legislation if passed would achieve this goal since jurisdiction is vested in the state courts (and federal courts in diversity of state citizenship cases)[94] with little likelihood of the United States Supreme Court imposing uniformity through the exercise of its certiorari jurisdiction.

Apparently the actual reason for the proposed legislation is to retrench significantly on plaintiffs' rights in products litigation. The reason in turn for this effort is because of a widespread concern among manufacturers over soaring products liability insurance premiums.[95] However, the reasons for these admittedly substantial increased rates within the past half-dozen years have by no means been clearly identified.[96] It would seem that such identification would be a condition precedent to the enactment of such far-reaching legislation.

## FOOTNOTES

1    *Vlases v Montgomery Ward & Co*, 377 F 2d 846 (3d Cir, 1967).

2    *Gaston v Hunter*, 121 Ariz 33, 588 P 2d 326 (1978).

3    (k) Unavoidably unsafe products. There are some products which, in the present state of human knowledge, are quite incapable of being made safe for their intended and ordinary use. These are especially common in the field of drugs. An outstanding example is the vaccine for the Pasteur treatment of rabies, which not uncommonly leads to very serious and damaging consequences when it is injected. Since the disease itself invariably leads to a dreadful death, both the marketing and the use of the vaccine are fully justified, notwithstanding the unavoidable high degree of risk which they involve. Such a product, properly prepared, and accompanied by proper directions and warning, is not defective, nor is it unreasonably dangerous The same is true of many other drugs, vaccines, and the like, many of which for this very reason

cannot legally be sold except to physicians, or under the prescription of a physician. It is also true in particular of many new or experimental drugs as to which, because of lack of time and opportunity for sufficient medical experience, there can be no assurance of safety or perhaps even of purity of ingredients, but such experience as there is justifies the marketing and use of the drug notwithstanding a medically recognizable risk. The seller of such products, again with the qualification that they are properly prepared and marketed, and proper warning is given, where the situation calls for it, is not to be held to strict liability for unfortunate consequences attending their use, merely because he has undertaken to supply the public with an apparently useful and desirable product, attended with a known but apparently reasonable risk.

4    Comment (k) applied to sunglasses, *Filler v Rayex Corp*, 435 F 2d 336 (7th Cir, 1970); to asbestos, *Borel v Fibreboard Paper Products Corp*, 493 F 2d 1076 (5th Cir, 1973).

5    See *Phillipe v Browning Arms*, 375 So 2d 151 (La App, 1979), design and production in defect equated (design method of hand-bending safety pins in guns resulting in random defect).

6    *Bowman v General Motors Corp*, 427 F Supp 234 (E D Pa, 1977).

7    See Comment, 50 Tenn L Rev 515 (1983).

8    *Balido v Improved Machinery, Inc*, 29 Cal App 3d 633, 105 Cal Rptr 890 (1973). However, "a retailer, wholesaler, or other supplier who takes no part in the design of the product is clearly not likely to be negligent". D Noel and J Phillips, *Products Liability* 140 (2d ed, 1981).

9    *Roach v Kononen*, 525 P 2d 125 (Ore, 1974).

10   *Borel v Fibreboard Paper Products Corp*, 493 F 2d 1076 (5th Cir, 1973).

11   *Barker v Lull Engineering Co*, 20 Cal 3d 413, 143 Cal Rptr 225, 573 P 2d 443 (1978).

12   Idem. And see *Kelly v R G Industries, Inc*, CCH Prod Liab Rptr par 10,669 (Md App, 1985) (manufacturers of "Saturday Night Specials" handguns may be held strictly liable for injuries resulting from criminal misuse of such guns, which lack any social utility).

13 *O'Brien v Muskin Corp*, 94 NJ 169, 463 A 2d 298 (1983).

14 *Woodill v Parke Davis & Co*, 79 Ill 2d 26, 402 NE 2d 194 (1980).

15 *Bryant v Hercules Inc*, 325 F Supp 241 (W D Ky, 1970).

16 *Baxter v Ford Motor Co*, 179 Wash 123, 35 P 2d 1090 (1934).

17 *Winkler v Amer Safety Equip Corp*, 640 P 2d 216 (Colo, 1982), no recovery because of absence of proof of reliance. But see *Sterner v US Plywood-Champion Paper, Inc*, 519 F 2d 1352 (8th Cir, 1975), advertisement unseen by plaintiff goes to the issue of intended use and product's unfitness therefor; *Hiller v Kawasaki Motors*, 671 P 2d 369 (Alas, 1983), post-injury snow-mobile-jump advertisements relevant to issue of foreseeable use. Comment (j) to para 402B of the Second Restatement of Torts, dealing with inno-cent tortious misrepresentation, states that the reliance need not be that of the plaintiff but may consist of reliance by the purchaser who passes the product along to the plaintiff.

18 *Gertz v Robert Welch, Inc*, 418 US 323 (1974).

19 *Garrison v Lan*, 85 S Ct 209 (1964) (constitu-tional protection for private individual using the media); *Harley-Davidson Motorsports v Markley*, 279 Ore 361, 568 P 2d 1359 (1977) (no constitutional protection for non-medium defendant, private plaintiff, and matter not involving public interest).

20 *Jacron Sales Co v Sindorf*, 276 Md 580, 350 A 2d 688 (1976).

21 See Phillips "Product Misrepresentation and the First Amendment", 18 Idaho L Rev 395 (1982).

22 *Bose Corp v Consumers Union of US, Inc*, 692 F 2d 189 (1st Cir, 1982), aff'd 104 S Ct 1949 (1984).

23 [1868] LR, 3 HL 330.

24 See *Cities Serv Co v State*, 312 So 2d 799 (Fla, 1975) (phosphate sludge pond); *Siegler v Kuhlman*, 91 Wash 2d 448, 502 P 2d 1181 (1972) (gasoline truck); *Richman v Charter Arms*, 571 F Supp 192 (E D La, 1983) (handgun).

25 D Noel and J Phillips, *Products Liability Cases and Materials* 94-111 (2d ed, 1982).

26    *Elmore v American Motors Corp*, 70 Cal ed 578, 75 Cal Rptr 652, 452 P 2d 84 (1969).

27    Eg, *Walker v Clark Equip Co*, 320 N W 2d 561 (Iowa, 1982), recovery for emotional distress in witnessing injury caused by defective product; *Guarino v Mine Safety Appl Co*, 25 NY 2d 460, 306 NYS 2d 942, 255 NE 2d 173 (1969), rescuer recovery.

28    *Star Furniture Co v Pulaski Furniture Co*, 297 SE 2d 854 (W Va, 1982).

29    *Cinnaminson Township Board of Education v U S Gypsum Co*, 552 F Supp 855 (NJ, 1982), moving asbestos foam insulation from public building constitutes physical harm.

30    *Fordyce Concrete v Reynbolds Metals*, 535 F Supp 118 (D C Kan, 1982).

31    *Borel v Fibreboard Paper Products Corp*, 493 F 2d 1076 (5th Cir, 1973).

32    *Seely v White Motor Co*, 63 Cal 2d 9, 45 Cal Rptr 17, 403 P 2d 145 (1965).

33    Idem.

34    Idem dissenting opinion.

35    See Annotation, 91 ALR 3d 921 (1979), on products liability insurance coverage.

36    See S 44, 98th Cong, 1st Sess, 129 Congr Rec S 284 (daily ed 26 Jan 1983); 5 L Frumer and M Friedman Appendix H, State Products Liability Legislation (1982).

37    See Shapo, "Representational Theory", 60 Va L Rev 1109 (1974).

38    See *World-Wide Volkswagen Corp v Woodson* 444 US, 286 (1980).

39    "Recent estimates [by the Environmental Protection Agency] place the number of potentially dangerous hazardous waste sites [in the United States] at 22,000." BNA Envir Rep p. 2308 (15 Apr 1983).

40    See comments 36 Vand L Rev 573 (1983); 11 Pepperdine L Rev 125 (1983); idem at 151.

41    Idem,

42    *Sindell v Abbott Laboratories*, 26 Cal 3d 588, 163 Cal Rptr 132, 607 P 2d 924 (1980).

43    *Hammon v Waterman Steamship Co*, 567 F Supp 90 (E D La, 1983) (asbestos).

44    *Sindell*, note 42 *supra*.

45    *Bichler v Eli Lilly & Co*, 55 N Y 2d 571, 450 N
      Y S 2d 776 (1982).

46    *Collins v Eli Lilly Co*, 342 N W 2d 47 (Wis,
      1984).

47    *Landers v East Texas Salt Water Disp. Co*, 248
      S W 2d 731 (Tex, 1952).

48    *Atl Veterans Transp Inc v Cagle*, 127 S E 2d
      702 (Ga App, 1962).

49    *Payton v Abbott Laboratories*, 437 N E 2d 171
      (Mass, 1982).

50    Comment, 36 Vand L Rev 573 (1983).

51    See Comment, 97 Harv L Rev 739 (1984).

52    *Keene Corp v Ins Co of North America*, 677 F 2d
      1034 (D C Cir, 1981).

53    Phillips, "Asbestos Litigation", 36 Ark L Rev
      343, 358-359 (1982).

54    *Jackson v Johns-Manville Sales Corp*, No
      82-4288 (5th Cir, 23 March, 1984).

55    *Wangen v Ford Motor Co*, 294 N W 2d 437 (Wis,
      1980).

56    *Grimshaw v Ford Motor Co*, 119 Cal App 3d 757,
      174 Cal Rptr 348 (1981).

57    This approach was suggested in dictum in
      *Roginsky v Richardson-Merrell, Inc*, 378 F 2d
      832 (2d Cir, 1967).

58    *Michael v Cole*, 595 P 2d 995 (Ariz, 1979).

59    Comment, 44 J Air Law & Commerce 1, 14 (1978).

60    C. McCormick, *Damages*, 278-279 (1935).

61    *Alvis v Ribar*, 421 N E 2d 886 (Ill, 1981).

62    L Prosser et al, *Cases and Materials on Torts*,
      610 (7th ed, 1982).

63    D Noel and J Phillips, *Cases and Materials on
      Torts and Related Law*, 343 (1980).

64    *Sandford v General Motors Corp*, 642 P 2d 624
      (Ore, 1982).

65    *Coney v JLG Industries*, 454 N E 2d 197 (Ill,
      1983).

66    Id.

67    *Mtn Mobile Mix v Gifford*, 660 P 2d 883 (Colo,
      1983).

68 Tennessee, for example, has remote comparative negligence based on degrees of fault, (*Reid v US*, 447 F 2d 275 (6th Cir, 1971)), but contribution among defendants is apportioned on an equal-share basis, Tenn Code Annot para 29-11-103 (1980).

69 Weisgall, "Product Liability in the Workplace", (1977) Wis L Rev 1035, 1038-1039.

70 *Arctic Structures, Inc v Wedmore*, 605 P 2d 426, 439-440 (Alas, 1979).

71 See Phillips, "Successor Corporation Liability", 58 N Y U L Rev 906 (1983).

72 *Ray v Alad Corp*, 19 Cal 3d 33, 560 P 2d 3, 136 Cal Rptr 574 (1977); *Turner v Bitum Cas Co*, 397 Mich 406, 244 N W 2d 873 (1976).

73 See *Tift v Forage King Indus*, 108 Wis 2d 72, 322 N W 2d 14 (1982).

74 See Phillips *supra* note 71, at 921-922.

75 Idem.

76 *Phillips v Kimwood Machine Co*, 269 Ore 485, 525 P 2d 1033 (1974).

77 *Roach v Kononen*, 525 P 2d 125 (1974).

78 *Sindell v Abbot Laboratories*, 607 P 2d 924 (Cal, 1980).

79 *Anderson v Somberg*, 67 N J 291, 338 A 2d 1 (1975).

80 *Halstead v US*, 535 F Supp 782 (D C Conn, 1982) (navigational chart).

81 *Avner v Longridge Estates*, 272 Cal App 2d 607, 77 Cal Rptr 633 (1969).

82 *Garcia v Halsett*, 3 Cal App 3d 319, 82 Cal Rptr 420 (1970).

83 *Davis v Gibson Products Co*, 505 S W 2d 682 (Tex Civ App, 1973).

84 *Becker v IRM Corp*, 144 Cal App 3d 321 (1983).

85 *Hempstead v Gen'l Fire Exting Corp*, 269 F Supp 109 (D C Del, 1967) (tester); *Kosters v Seven-up Co*, 595 F 2d 347 (6th Cir, 1979) (franchiser); *City of Hartford v Assoc Construction Co*, 34 Conn Super 204, 384 A 2d 390 (1978) (licenser).

86 See *Tamarac Develop v Delameter, Freund & Assoc*, 675 P 2d 361 (Kan, 1984); Green, "The Duty to Give Accurate Information", 12 UCLA L Rev 464 (1965).

87 Smith, "Sequel to Workmen's Compensation Acts", 27 Harv L Rev 344, 363 (1914).

88 See T Ison, *Accident Compensation - a Commentary on the New Zealand Scheme* (1980).

89 J O'Connell, *Ending Insult to Injury* 73-76 (1975).

90 See Vandall, "Products Liability Legislation", 30 Amer U L Rev 673 (1981).

91 See Phillips, "The Proposed Federal Products Liability Statute" 28 Vill L Rev 1156 (1982-1983).

92 Idem.

93 Report of Senate Comm, S 2631, 97th Cong 2d Sess, 128 Cong Rec 6878 (1982).

94 S 2631, para 3(d); accord S 44, *supra* note 36.

95 See Interagency Task Force Report, Nat Tech Info Serv (GPO 1977).

96 Idem.

# THE LAW OF PRODUCTS LIABILITY IN THE COMMON LAW PROVINCES OF CANADA

*S.M. Waddams*

## 1.   The Common Law Background

(a)   <u>Negligence</u>.   The   principal   basis   of   liability
for   damage   caused   by   defective   products   is   negli-[1]*
gence.      Ths Scottish case of *Donoghue v Stevenson,*
holding   that   a   manufacturer   of   products   owes   a   duty
of   care   to   the   ultimate   consumer,   has   been   accepted
in   Canada,   and   the   subsequent   extensions   of   the
principle   in   the   leading   Commonwealth   cases   have   also
been   adopted.

In   theory,   the   plaintiff is required to prove
fault,   but   the   rule   of   vicarious   liability,   whereby
an employer is liable for his employees' wrongs, combined with a willingness to infer negligence from the
existence   of   a   defect   in   a   product,   has   a   practical
effect   that   approaches   strict   liability.   In   a   leading   Australian   case   involving   injury   caused   by   excess
sulphites   in   underwear,   the   Privy   Council   said[2]:

"If   excess   sulphites were left in the garment,
that   could   only   be   because   someone   was   at   fault.
[The   plaintiff]   is   not   required   to   lay   his
finger   on the exact person in all the chain who
was   responsible,   or   to   specify   what   he   did
wrong.   Negligence   is   found   as   a   matter   of
inference   from   the   existence   of   the   defects
taken   in   conjunction with all the known circumstances."

In   a   more   recent   case   the   Ontario   High   Court   said:

"Where   the   defect   arises   in   the   manufacturing

---

\*     For   footnotes   see   p. 170

process controlled by the defendant the inference of negligence is practically irresistible
.... Either the manufacturer's system was at
fault or, if the system was sound, then an individual employee must have been negligent."[3]

Although the effect of these lines of reasoning,
as has been said, is to approach strict liability,
there remain a number of kinds of cases in which a
plaintiff can prove that he has been injured by a
defective product and yet fail to recover against a
supplier. The manufacturer may be able to show that,
though a defect subsequently became apparent, at the
time of manufacture or supply the defect could not
have been discovered by the use of reasonable care.
Secondly, where the product is defective because it
incorporates defective materials or components the
manufacturer of the completed product may escape
liability. Thirdly, the inference of negligence only
applies in full force to a manufacturer, not to other
suppliers such as wholesalers, retailers,
distributors, or importers, who will rarely be found
liable under a negligence regime.

(b) <u>Implied Warranties</u>. The second main branch of
the law of products liability depends on implied
warranties in sales. Every common law jurisdiction
has inherited the United Kingdom Sale of Goods Act of
1893, which provides that a business seller of goods
warrants that the goods are merchantable and reasonably fit for the buyer's purpose. The theory is
contractual but the warranties do not depend on any
real promise by the seller. The effect is to impose
strict liability on the business seller for injuries
caused by defects. Several recent Canadian cases
have affirmed that the seller is liable for personal
injuries without proof of negligence.[4]

Regarded from the point of view of strict liability, however, the contractual basis of warranty
liability leads to severe anomalies. Only the buyer
is protected: thus where the cap flies off a soda
water bottle and injures the buyer's eye, the buyer
can recover,[5] but if the injury occurs to his wife or
child[6] or to a visitor there can be no recovery
against the retailer based on warranty. A sale, or
at least a contract,[7] is required: thus a shopper
injured in a store by an exploding bottle will have
no warranty claim against the retailer,[8] though if he
is injured just the other side of the cash register
the retailer will be liable. Further, it is
anomalous to impose strict liability on the retailer
but to hold the manufacturer, usually the party
primarily responsible for the defect, to the more

lenient standard of negligence.

(c) Strict Liability in Tort. A few cases have openly imposed strict liability in tort, and some of these involve products.[9] No general principle of strict liability for defective products has, however, evolved.

(d) Breach of Statute. In some Commonwealth juris-dictions liability for breach of statutory standards has supplied a means of imposing strict liability. This line of reasoning, however, has not been accepted in Canada, where the Supreme Court of Canada has recently affirmed that a breach of statute does not, in the absence of negligence, generally lead to liability.[10]

(e) Mis-statements. In some cases injury is caused, not by a defect in the product itself, but by a misleading statement. Where the statement accom-panies the product, as in the case of inadequate instructions on the package, the product, taken as a whole, can be held to be defective. Where, however, the statement is made separately, for example in a manufacturer's handbook, this analysis is not available. Where negligence can be shown, the statement will be actionable in negligence.[11] Where negligence is not shown, the statement may be actionable as a warranty. Even where the plaintiff and defendant are not in any apparent contractual relationship, a collateral contract may be constructed.[12] This theory, however, still would probably[13] require proof by the plaintiff that he relied on the defendant's statement in purchasing the product, and therefore falls short of a general principle of strict liability.

## 2.    Consumer Protection Legislation

(a) Saskatchewan. In Saskatchewan the Consumer Pro-ducts Warranties Act, 1977, largely based on a report of the Ontario Law Reform Commission,[14] enacts certain non-excludable statutory warranties that apply in all consumer sales. These include warran-ties of acceptable quality, reasonable fitness for the buyer's purpose, and a warranty of durability. An action for breach of the warranties may be brought not only against the retailer seller, but also against the manufacturer. The term "manufacturer" is defined to include any person who attaches his brand name to consumer products, any person who describes himself or holds himself out to the public as the manufacturer, and any person who imports products where the manufacturer does not have a regular place

of business in Canada. Section 5 of this Act provides as follows:

> "A person who may reasonably be expected to use,
> consume or be affected by a consumer product and
> who suffers personal injury as a result of a
> breach, by a retail seller or manufacturer, of a
> statutory warranty mentioned in paragraphs 3, 4,
> 5 and 6 of section 11 shall be entitled to the
> remedies mentioned in section 27."[15]

Section 27 provides:

> "A person mentioned in Section 5 shall, as
> against the retail seller or manufacturer, be
> entitled to recover damages arising from per-
> sonal injuries that he has suffered and that
> were reasonably foreseeable as liable to result
> from the breach."

These sections are restricted to claims for personal
injuries. In relation to such claims, however, the
effect of these sections is greatly to extend the
strict liability of distributors of goods, and to
resolve the most striking anomalies mentioned above.
This enactment brings the law of Saskatchewan very
close to adopting a general rule of strict liability.
In many of the examples given above, where an injured
plaintiff might fail to recover under common law
because of the absence of a contract or the inability
to establish negligence, he would succeed under the
present law of Saskatchewan. Nevertheless, there are
a few respects in which the Saskatchewan Act falls
short of a general rule of strict liability.

First, the Act only applies to consumer products, defined as goods ordinarily used for personal,
family, or household purposes, or for agricultural or
fishing purposes. This restriction sets up a
distinction that may well be justifiable where the
consumer's complaint is of deficient value. The
distinction does not, however, appear to be
acceptable in the case of personal injuries. A
coin-operated dryer, manufactured for use in a coin
laundry, for instance, is probably not a "consumer
product" within the statutory definition. But if a
user is injured by a faulty electrical connection in
such a dryer, should he not be entitled to compensation? Again, the statutory warranties only apply
where a consumer product "is sold by a retail
seller". A retail seller is defined as a person who
sells consumer products to consumers in the ordinary
course of his business. The person injured by the
coin-operated dryer would also be excluded on this

ground.    So too would the pedestrian injured by the
failure  of  defective  brakes  on  a truck owned and
operated  by a business user.   Also excluded would be
the  shopper  injured in a supermarket before purchase
of  a  defective  product.   In none of these cases is
the  product  "sold  by  a  retail  seller".    These
restrictions   seem  anomalous,  for  where  personal
injuries  are  in question, it does not seem relevant
to ask either whether the defective product is a consumer product or whether it has been sold by a retail
seller.    The  rights  of  the  injured plaintiff to
recover  damages  are  restricted  by  reference to a
transaction  that  appears irrelevant to the question
of compensation for such injuries.

There  are some other respects, though they cannot  be  described as anomalies, in which the Saskatchewan  Act  falls  short of a general rule of strict
liability  such  as  that  applied  in  most American
jurisdictions  by  the  judicial  adoption of section
402A  of  the Restatement (Second) of Torts.  Section
402A  imposes  liability  on  any  business seller of
goods.   The Saskatchewan Act is restricted to certain
classes  of  business distributor, and  does  not
include,  for  example,  the  wholesaler,  except  in
certain  circumstances.[16]    Nor would, for example, a
business  lessor  always  be  included.[17]   Again, the
extended  liability applies only to personal injures;
unlike  section  402A,  the Saskatchewan Act does not
apply to property damage, nor does it apply to purely
economic loss.

(b)  New  Brunswick.    The main part of the Consumer
Product  Warranty  and  Liability  Act 1978  provides
non-excludable  warranties  in sales of consumer products,  and extends a remedy for breach to any person
suffering a non-business loss.   Section 27 of the Act
goes  further.    It creates a direct strict liability
for  the  supply  of  dangerously defective products.
The  section  is  entitled  "Product Liability" and
provides as follows:

"(1)    A  supplier of a consumer product that is
unreasonably  dangerous  to  person  or property
because  of  a  defect  in  design, materials or
workmanship  is liable to any person who suffers
a  consumer  loss in the Province because of the
defect,  if  the loss was reasonably foreseeable
at  the  time  of his supply as liable to result
from the defect and

(a)    he  has  supplied the consumer product in
the Province:
(b)    he  has  supplied  the  consumer  product

                outside the Province but has done something in the Province that contributes to the consumer loss suffered in the Province; or

(c)        he has supplied the consumer product outside the Province but the defect arose in whole or in part because of his failure to comply with any mandatory federal standards in relation to health or safety, or the defect caused the consumer product to fail to comply with any such standards.

(2)    For the purposes of paragraph (1)(b), where a person has done anything in the Province to further the supply of any consumer product that is similar in kind to the consumer product that caused the loss, it shall be presumed that he has done something in the Province that contributed to the consumer loss suffered in the Province, unless he proves irrefragably that what he did in the Province did not in any way contribute to that loss.

(3)    A person is not liable under this section

(a)        for any loss that is caused by a defect that is not present in the consumer product at the time he supplies it: or

(b)        for any loss that is caused by a defect that he has reason to believe exists and that he discloses to the person to whom he supplies the consumer product before the loss is suffered, if the defect does not arise in whole or in part because of his failure to comply with any mandatory federal or provincial standards in relation to health or safety and the defect does not cause the consumer product to fail to comply with any such standards.

(4)    The liability of a person under this section does not depend on any contract or negligence."

"Consumer loss" and "consumer product" are defined in section 1(1) of the Act as follows:

"'consumer loss' means

(a)        a loss that a person does not suffer in a business capacity; or

(b)        a loss that a person suffers in a busi-

> ness capacity to the extent that it con-
> sists of liability that he or another
> person incurs for a loss that is not
> suffered in a business capacity;
>
> 'consumer product' means any tangible personal
> property, new or used, of a kind that is com-
> monly used for personal, family or household
> purposes."

Section 27 and the definitions set out above go considerably beyond the provisions of the Saskatchewan
Act. It will be noted that they apply to all business suppliers of products, including wholesalers,
and that they cover some non-business property damage
and economic losses as well as personal injury.
Further, in the case of safety related defects, no
contract at all is necessary. However, like the
Saskatchewan provisions, these provisions seems to be
restricted to consumer goods. Thus, the user injured
by a defective coin laundry appliance, or a pedestrian injured by a defective truck owned and operated by a business user, would seem to be without
protection. Similarly, a shopper injured by a defective plate glass window, or a defective display
shelving unit (not being of a type ordinarily used by
consumers) would be without a remedy under these
provisions.

(c) <u>Safety Standards Legislation</u>. A number of
federal statutes deal with product standards. It is
doubtful whether a breach of these statutes is itself
enough to establish liability for damage caused by
defects.[18] However, in the Saskatchewan Consumer
Products Warranties Act it is provided that proof of
non-compliance with mandatory health or safety
standards or with quality standards constitutes prima
facie evidence that the consumer product is of
acceptable quality or fit for the purpose for which
it was bought. The New Brunswick Consumer Warranty
and Liability Act 1978 provides in section 27(1)(c)
that a manufacturer who supplies a product outside
the province is liable for defects caused by
non-compliance with federal statutory standards.

3.   Ontario Law Reform Commission Report of 1979
     (Appendix C, p. 193)

In 1979 the Ontario Law Reform Commission publisheda
report on products liability, which recommended the
enactment of a principle of liability that would
apply to business suppliers of defective products
without proof of fault and without the need to establish a contractual relationship. In other words,
the proposal was for a principle of strict liability
in tort.

The main thrust of the reasoning supporting the Commission's proposal was one of rationalizing the existing law. Strict liability already exists in large measure, by inferences of negligence drawn from the existence of a defect, and by warranties in sales law. However, as has been pointed out, the principle is subject to anomalous restrictions. The only way of rationalizing the existing law of negligence with the law of implied warranties was, as it seemed to the Commission, to make all business suppliers strictly liable. Proof of a defect would still be required, so the number of cases in which the result reached under the present law would be changed could be expected to be small. A parallel provision was proposed to impose strict liability on business suppliers for damage caused by reliance on false statements about products.

On the difficult question of the kinds of losses to be recoverable, the Commission recommended that personal injury and non-business property loss only should be included. Thus business property loss and pure economic loss were excluded. The question of economic loss and the relationship of such loss to contractual expectations and to contractual exemption clauses is one on which opinions differ, and in fact two of the Commissioners dissented on the point. In view of the limited scope of the majority recommendation, the Commission had no difficulty in concluding that exemption clauses should be wholly ineffective. It should be pointed out that the Commission's proposals were supplementary to the existing law, and would not impede any common law development towards recovery of economic loss in negligence.

The proposals include a right on the part of any supplier held liable to claim over against any prior supplier who would, if sued, also have been liable. Thus the retailer, for example, does not take the ultimate risk of liability, though he does take the risk of finding the manufacturer and prior suppliers unknown, insolvent, or beyond the jurisdiction.

The Commission's proposals recommend, as has been said, a comparatively modest change in the law. The basic system of individual responsibility would continue. Proof of defect and causation would still be required, and, as has been said, it is unlikely that the Commission's recommendations would alter the result of many cases. More radical proposals are made from time to time that would introduce a general state supported system of accident compensation as in New Zealand, but would not depend on how the accident was caused.[19] Such a scheme could not rationally be limited to injuries caused by products, but would presumably include such injuries. Quebec has adopted a general compensation scheme that displaces tort law for automobile injuries. There does not appear, however, to be any great likelihood of a scheme along the lines of the New Zealand scheme being enacted in the Canadian common law provinces in the immediate future.

## 4.   Conflicts of Provincial Laws

The conflicts questions in products liability are potentially quite complex. The current position is approximately as follows. The provinces generally have wide jurisdictional rules and narrow recognition and enforcement rules.[20] Choice of law rules generally require a tort to be actionable by the law of the forum and not justifiable by the law of the place of the tort. The Ontario Law Reform Commission Report of 1979 adopted a comparatively simple approach to the conflicts questions, based on the underlying notion that a supplier who benefits from the marketplace of another jurisdiction than his own (i.e., in the context of the report, Ontario) should be prepared to submit to the process and to the law of that jurisdiction (Ontario).

Where legislation is contemplated for a single province, the inevitable tendency is to recommend wide jurisdictional rules and narrow rules for recognition and enforcement of extra-provincial judgments. Ideally, judgments of sister Canadian provinces should be recognized and enforced on some basis similar to the American "full faith and credit" rule. But since this ideal state of affairs is unlikely soon to be realized, a single province is bound to favour wide jurisdiction for its own courts and narrow recognition of extra-provincial judgments. It is for this reason that the Ontario report included no recommendation on recognition.

From a national point of view, however, a wider perspective is required. There are very strong reasons for favouring uniform legislation on products liability, and the Uniform Law Conference of Canada recommended in 1984 a uniform Act based on the Ontario Law Reform Commission Report, but with some significant changes. Judgments given under the uniform Act would be enforceable in all provinces that had adopted the Act.

The Ontario Law Reform Commission and the Uniform Law Conference proposed, for purposes of jurisdiction, a test based on "carrying on business" in the province with this phrase defined to include any case where the product or identical products supplied by the supplier were available or accessible in the province through commercial channels with the supplier's consent or foresight, or where the supplier had acted in any way to further the supply of the product in the province. This approach is capable of offering, it is suggested, a rational and coherent test both for jurisdiction and enforcement. The basis would be that one who chooses to carry on business in a jurisdiction ought to be answerable to an action brought by a person injured there.

The Ontario Law Reform Commission Report and the Uniform Law Conference adopted the same test (i.e. carrying on business as defined above) for choice of law, providing that Ontario law should apply in any case where the supplier had carried on business in Ontario. Very complex and widely divergent tests have been suggested for choice of law in products liability.[21] The main objection to the Ontario proposal would be that it does not give to the plaintiff the choice, which some other formulations would give him, of a more favourable foreign law, for example the law of the defendant's principal place of business. The force of this objection is, however, diminished, though not wholly overcome, in the context of a statute enacting a change in domestic law favourable to plaintiffs, for it can be said that the plaintiff will less often than formerly be more favourably treated under the law of a foreign defendant's place of business than under domestic law.

In conclusion it should be noted that the history of attempts at uniform legislation in Canada cannot justify a very great optimism about the early enactment of legislation.

## FOOTNOTES

1    [1932] AC 562 (HL.SC).

2    *Grant v Australian Knitting Mills Ltd* [1936] AC 85 (PC) at 101.

3    *McMorran v Dominion Stores Ltd* (1977) 14 DLR (3d) 186 (Ont HC).

4    *McMorran v Dominion Stores Ltd.,* supra note 3; *Sigurdson v Hillcrest Service Ltd* (1977) 73 DLR

(3d) 132 (Sask QB); *Brunski v Dominion Stores Ltd* (1981) 20 CCLT 14 (Ont HC); *Leitz v Saskatoon Drug & Stationery Co Ltd* (1980) 112 DLR (3d) 106 (Sask QB).

5   *McMorran v Dominion Stores Ltd*, supra note 3.

6   See *Sigurdson v Hillcrest Service Ltd*, supra note 4.

7   Implied warranties have been incorporated by analogy into various non-sale transactions. See, for example, *Hart v Bell Telephone Co of Canada Ltd* (1979) 102 DLR (3d) 465 (Ont CA) where a telephone company was held strictly liable for injury to a user by electric shock.

8   See *Hart v Dominion Stores Ltd* (1968) 67 DLR (2d) 675 (Ont HC).

9   *Shiffman v Order of St. John* [1936] 1 All ER 557 (KB); *Hale v Jennings Bros* [1938] 1 All ER 579; *MacDonald v Desourdy Const Ltee* (1972) 27 DLR (3d) 144 (NSTD); *Mihalchuk v Ratke* (1966) 57 DLR (2d) 269 (Sask QB).

10  *R v Saskatchewan Wheat Pool* (1983) 143 DLR (3d) 9 (SCC).

11  *Robson v Chrysler Corp of Canada Ltd* (1962) 32 DLR (2d) 49 (Alta App Div); *Clayton v Woodman & Son (Builders) Ltd* [1962] 2 QB 533 (CA) leave to appeal refused [1962] 1 WLR 920 (HL); *Clay v A J Crump & Sons Ltd* [1964] 1 QB 533 (CA).

12  *Andrews v Hopkinson* [1957] 1 QB 229; *Murray v Sperry Rand Corp* (1979) 96 DLR (3d) 113.

13  Possibly it might be argued that use of the product constituted a sufficient consideration for the defendant's promise.

14  Report on Consumer Warranties and Guarantees in the Sale of Goods, Ontario Law Reform Commission 1972.

15  Paragraphs 3, 4 and 5 of s 11 correspond to the warranties of description, acceptable quality and reasonable fitness of purpose.

16  A wholesaler is included within the definition of manufacturer if he attaches a brand name to a product, holds himself out to the public as the manufacturer, or imports or distributes products of foreign manufacture.

17  Under s 2(m) the definition of "sale" includes a contract of lease or hire, but is restricted to cases where the seller "transfers or agrees to transfer the general property" in a product.

18    See supra note 10.

19    See E  P  Belobaba, *Products Liability and  Per-
      sonal  Injury  Compensation  in  Canada:  Towards
      integration  and rationalization.* Department   of
      Consumer and Corporate Affairs, Ottawa, 1983.

20    See   Sharpe, *Interprovincial  Product  Liability
      Litigation,* Butterworths, Toronto, 1982.

21    See Sharpe, *op.cit.* supra, note 20, 77-109.

## APPENDIX A

COUNCIL DIRECTIVE

of 25 July 1985

on the approximation of the laws, regulations
and administrative provisions of the
Member States concerning liability
for defective products

(85/374/EEC)

THE COUNCIL OF THE EUROPEAN COMMUNITIES,

Having regard to the Treaty establishing the European
Economic Community, and in particular Article 100
thereof,

Having regard to the proposal from the Commission.[1][*]

Having regard to the opinion of the European Parliament.[2]

Having regard to the opinion of the Economic and
Social Committee.[3]

Whereas approximation of the laws of the Member
States concerning the liability of the producer for
damage caused by the defectiveness of his products is
necessary because the existing divergences may
distort competition and affect the movement of goods
within the common market and entail a differing
degree of protection of the consumer against damage
caused by a defective product to his health or property;

Whereas liability without fault on the part of the

---

[*]    For footnotes see p. 183

producer is the sole means of adequately solving the problem, peculiar to our age of increasing technicality, of a fair apportionment of the risks inherent in modern technological production;

Whereas liability without fault should apply only to movables which have been industrially produced; whereas, as a result, it is appropriate to exclude liability for agricultural products and game, except where they have undergone a processing of an industrial nature which could cause a defect in those products; whereas the liability provided for in this Directive should also apply to movables which are used in the construction of immovables or are installed in immovables;

Whereas protection of the consumer requires that all producers involved in the production process should be made liable, in so far as their finished product, component part or any raw material supplied by them was defective; whereas, for the same reason, liability should extend to importers of products into the Community and to persons who present themselves as producers by affixing their name, trade mark or other distinguishing feature or who supply a product the producer of which cannot be identified;

Whereas, in situations where several persons are liable for the same damage, the protection of the consumer requires that the injured person should be able to claim full compensation for the damage from any one of them;

Whereas, to protect the physical well-being and property of the consumer, the defectiveness of the product should be determined by reference not to its fitness for use but to the lack of the safety which the public at large is entitled to expect; whereas the safety is assessed by excluding any misuse of the product not reasonable under the circumstances;

Whereas a fair apportionment of risk between the injured person and the producer implies that the producer should be able to free himself from liability if he furnishes proof as to the existence of certain exonerating circumstances;

Whereas the protection of the consumer requires that the liability of the producer remains unaffected by acts or omissions of other persons having contributed to cause the damage; whereas, however, the contributory negligence of the injured person may be taken into account to reduce or disallow such liability;

Whereas the protection of the consumer requires compensation for death and personal injury as well as
compensation for damage to property; whereas the
latter should nevertheless be limited to goods for
private use or consumption and be subject to a deduc-
tion of a lower threshold of a fixed amount in order
to avoid litigation in an excessive number of cases;
whereas this Directive should not prejudice compensation for pain and suffering and other non-material
damages payable, where appropriate, under the law
applicable to the case;

Whereas a uniform period of limitation for the bringing of action for compensation is in the interests
both of the injured person and of the producer;

Whereas products age in the course of time, higher
safety standards are developed and the state of
science and technology progresses; whereas, therefore, it would not be reasonable to make the producer
liable for an unlimited period for the defectiveness
of his product; whereas, therefore, liability should
expire after a reasonable length of time, without
prejudice to claims pending at law;

Whereas, to achieve effective protection of consumers, no contractual derogation should be permitted
as regards the liability of the producer in relation
to the injured person;

Whereas under the legal systems of the Member States
an injured party may have a claim for damages based
on grounds of contractual liability or on grounds of
non-contractual liability other than that provided
for in this Directive; in so far as these provisions
also serve to attain the objective of effective
protection of consumers, they should remain unaffected by this Directive; whereas, in so far as effective protection of consumers in the sector of pharmaceutical products is already also attained in a
Member State under a special liability system, claims
based on this system should similarly remain
possible;

Whereas, to the extent that liability for nuclear
injury or damage is already covered in all Member
States by adequate special rules, it has been possible to exclude damage of this type from the scope of
this Directive;

Whereas, since the exclusion of primary agricultural
products and game from the scope of this Directive
may be felt, in certain Member States, in view of
what is expected for the protection of consumers, to

restrict unduly such protection, it should be possible for a Member State to extend liability to such products;

Whereas, for similar reasons, the possibility offered to a producer to free himself from liability if he proves that the state of scientific and technical knowledge at the time when he put the product into circulation was not such as to enable the existence of a defect to be discovered may be felt in certain Member States to restrict unduly the protection of the consumer; whereas it should therefore be possible for a Member State to maintain in its legislation or to provide by new legislation that this exonerating circumstance is not admitted; whereas, in the case of new legislation, making use of this derogation should, however, be subject to a Community stand-still procedure, in order to raise, if possible, the level of protection in a uniform manner throughout the Community;

Whereas, taking into account the legal traditions in most of the Member States, it is inappropriate to set any financial ceiling on the producer's liability without fault; whereas, in so far as there are, however, differing traditions, it seems possible to admit that a Member State may derogate from the principle of unlimited liability by providing a limit for the total liability of the producer for damage resulting from a death or personal injury and caused by identical items with the same defect, provided that this limit is established at a level sufficiently high to guarantee adequate protection of the consumer and the correct functioning of the common market;

Whereas the harmonization resulting from this cannot be total at the present stage, but opens the way towards greater harmonization; whereas it is therefore necessary that the Council receive at regular intervals, reports from the Commission on the application of this Directive, accompanied, as the case may be, by appropriate proposals;

Whereas it is particularly important in this respect that a re-examination be carried out of those parts of the Directive relating to the derogation open to the Member States, at the expiry of a period of sufficient length to gather practical experience on the effects of these derogations on the protection of consumers and on the functioning of the common market,

HAS ADOPTED THIS DIRECTIVE:

### Article 1

The producer shall be liable for damage caused by a defect in his product.

### Article 2

For the purpose of this Directive 'product' means all movables, with the exception of primary agricultural products and game, even though incorporated into another movable or into an immovable. 'Primary agricultural products' means the products of the soil, of stock-farming and of fisheries, excluding products which have undergone initial processing. 'Product' includes electricity.

### Article 3

1.   'Producer' means the manufacturer of a finished product, the producer of any raw material or the manufacturer of a component part and any person who, by putting his name, trade mark or other distinguishing feature on the product presents himself as its producer.

2.   Without prejudice to the liability of the producer, any person who imports into the Community a product for sale, hire, leasing or any form of distribution in the course of his business shall be deemed to be a producer within the meaning of this Directive and shall be responsible as a producer.

3.   Where the producer of the product cannot be identified, each supplier of the product shall be treated as its producer unless he informs the injured person, within a reasonable time, of the identity of the producer or of the person who supplied him with the product. The same shall apply, in the case of an imported product, if this product does not indicate the identity of the importer referred to in paragraph 2, even if the name of the producer is indicated.

### Article 4

The injured person shall be required to prove the damage, the defect and the causal relationship between defect and damage.

### Article 5

Where, as a result of the provisions of this Directive, two or more persons are liable for the same damage, they shall be liable jointly and severally, without prejudice to the provisions of national law concerning the rights of contribution or recourse.

*Article 6*

1. A product is defective when it does not provide the safety which a person is entitled to expect, taking all circumstances into account, including:

(a) the presentation of the product;

(b) the use to which it could reasonably be expected that the product would be put;

(c) the time when the product was put into circulation.

2. A product shall not be considered defective for the sole reason that a better product is subsequently put into circulation.

*Article 7*

The producer shall not be liable as a result of this Directive if he proves:

(a) that he did not put the product into circulation; or

(b) that, having regard to the circumstances, it is probable that the defect which caused the damage did not exist at the time when the product was put into circulation by him or that this defect came into being afterwards; or

(c) that the product was neither manufactured by him for sale or any form of distribution for economic purpose nor manufactured or distributed by him in the course of his business; or

(d) that the defect is due to compliance of the product with mandatory regulations issued by the public authorities; or

(e) that the state of scientific and technical knowledge at the time when he put the product into circulation was not such as to enable the existence of the defect to be discovered; or

(f) in the case of a manufacturer of a component, that the defect is attributable to the design of the product in which the component has been fitted or to the instructions given by the manufacturer of the product.

### Article 8

1.   Without prejudice to the provisions of national law concerning the right of contribution or recourse, the liability of the producer shall not be reduced when the damage is caused both by a defect in the product and by the act or omission of a third party.

2.   The liability of the producer may be reduced or disallowed when, having regard to all the circumstanes, the damage is caused both by a defect in the product and by the fault of the injured person or any person for whom the injured person is responsible.

### Article 9

For the purpose of Article 1, 'damage' means:

(a)   damage caused by death or by personal injuries;

(b)   damage to, or destruction of, any item of property other than the defective product itself, with a lower threshold of 500 ECU, provided that the item of property:

   i.   is of a type ordinarily intended for private use or consumption, and

   ii.   was used by the injured person mainly for his own private use or consumption.

This Article shall be without prejudice to national provisions relating to non-material damage.

### Article 10

1.   Member States shall provide in their legislation that a limitation period of three years shall apply to proceedings for the recovery of damages as provided for in this Directive. The limitation period shall begin to run from the day on which the plaintiff became aware, or should reasonably have become aware, of the damage, the defect and the identity of the producer.

2.   The laws of Member States regulating suspension or interruption of the limitation period shall not be affected by this Directive.

*Article 11*

Member States shall provide in their legislation that the rights conferred upon the injured person pursuant to this Directive shall be extinguished upon the expiry of a period of 10 years from the date on which the producer put into circulation the actual product which caused the damage, unless the injured person has in the meantime instituted proceedings against the producer.

*Article 12*

The liability of the producer arising from this Directive may not, in relation to the injured person, be limited or excluded by a provision limiting his liability or exempting him from liability.

*Article 13*

This Directive shall not affect any rights which an injured person may have according to the rules of the law of contractual or non-contractual liability or a special liability system existing at the moment when this Directive is notified.

*Article 14*

This Directive shall not apply to injury or damage arising from nuclear accidents and covered by international conventions ratified by the Member States.

*Article 15*

1.　Each Member State may:

(a)　by way of derogation from Article 2, provide in its legislation that within the meaning of Article 1 of this Directive 'product' also means primary agricultural products and game;

(b)　by way of derogation from Article 7(e), maintain or, subject to the procedure set out in paragraph 2 of this Article, provide in this legislation that the producer shall be liable even if he proves that the state of scientific and technical knowledge at the time when he put the product into circulation was not such as to enable the existence of a defect to be discovered.

2.　A Member State wishing to introduce the measure specified in paragraph 1(b) shall communicate the text of the proposed measure to the Commission. The

Commission shall inform the other Member States thereof.

The Member State concerned shall hold the proposed measure in abeyance for nine months after the Commission is informed and provided that in the meantime the Commission has not submitted to the Council a proposal amending this Directive on the relevant matter. However, if within three months of receiving the said information, the Commission does not advise the Member State concerned that it intends submitting such a proposal to the Council, the Member State may take the proposed measure immediately.

If the Commission does submit to the Council such a proposal amending this Directive within the aforementioned nine months, the Member State concerned shall hold the proposed measure in abeyance for a further period of 18 months from the date on which the proposal is submitted.

3. Ten years after the date of notification of this Directive, the Commission shall submit to the Council a report on the effect that rulings by the courts as to the application of Article 7(e) and of paragraph 1(b) of this Article have on consumer protection and the functioning of the common market. In the light of this report the Council, acting on a proposal from the Commission and pursuant to the terms of Article 100 of the Treaty, shall decide whether to repeal Article 7(e).

*Article 16*

1. Any Member State may provide that a producer's total liability for damage resulting from a death or personal injury and caused by identical items with the same defect shall be limited to an amount which may not be less than 70 million ECU.

2. Ten years after the date of notification of this Directive, the Commission shall submit to the Council a report on the effect on consumer protection and the functioning of the common market of the implementation of the financial limit on liability by those Member States which have used the option provided for in paragraph 1. In the light of this report the Council, acting on a proposal from the Commission and pursuant to the terms of Article 100 of the Treaty, shall decide whether to repeal paragraph 1.

*Article 17*

This Directive shall not apply to products put into circulation before the date on which the provisions referred to in Article 19 enter into force.

*Article 18*

1. For the purposes of this Directive, the ECU shall be that defined by Regulation (EEC) No. 3180/78[4], as amended by Regulation (EEC) No. 2626/84[5]. The equivalent in national currency shall initially be calculated at the rate obtaining on the date of adoption of this Directive.

2. Every five years the Council, acting on a proposal from the Commission, shall examine and, if need be, revise the amounts in this Directive, in the light of economic and monetary trends in the Community.

*Article 19*

1. Member States shall bring into force, not later than three years from the date of notification of this Directive, the laws, regulations and administrative provisions necessary to comply with this Directive. They shall forthwith inform the Commission thereof.[6]

2. The procedure set out in Article 15(2) shall apply from the date of notification of this Directive.

*Article 20*

Member States shall communicate to the Commission the texts of the main provisions of national law which they subsequently adopt in the field governed by this Directive.

*Article 21*

Every five years the Commission shall present a report to the Council on the application of this Directive and, if necessary, shall submit appropriate proposals to it.

*Article 22*

This Directive is addressed to the Member States.

Done at Brussels, 25 July 1985.

**FOOTNOTES**

1.  OJ No C 241, 14.10.76, p 9 and OJ No C 271, 26.10.79, p 3.

2   OJ No C 127, 21.5.79, p 61.

3   OJ No C 114, 7.5.79, p 15.

4   OJ No L 379, 30.12.78, p 1.

5   OJ No L 247, 16.9.84, p 1.

6   This Directive was notified to the Member States on 30 July 1985.

## APPENDIX B

### European Convention on Products Liability in Regard to Personal Injury and Death

*Preamble*

The member States of the Council of Europe, signatories of this Convention,

Considering that the aim of the Council of Europe is to achieve a greater unity between its Members;

Considering the development of case law in the majority of Member States extending liability of producers prompted by a desire to protect consumers, taking into account the new production techniques and marketing and sales methods;

Desiring to ensure better protection of the public and at the same time, to take producers' legitimate interests into account;

Considering that a priority should be given to compensation for personal injury and death;

Aware of the importance of introducing special rules on the liability of producers at European level,

Have agreed as follows:[1]*

*Article 1*

1.   Each Contracting State shall make its national law conform with the provisions of this Convention not later than the date of the entry into force of the Convention in respect of that State.

---

\* For footnote see p. 191

2. Each Contracting State shall communicate to the Secretary General of the Council of Europe, not later than the date of the entry into force of the Convention in respect of that State, any text adopted or a statement of the contents of the existing law which it relies on to implement the Convention.

*Article 2*

For the purpose of this Convention:

(a) the term "product" indicates all movables, natural or industrial, whether raw or manufactured, even though incorporated into another movable or into an immovable;

(b) the term "producer" indicates the manufacturers of finished products or of component parts and the producers of natural products;

(c) a product has a "defect" when it does not provide the safety which a person is entitled to expect, having regard to all the circumstances including the presentation of the product;

(d) a product has been "put into circulation" when the producer has delivered it to another person.

*Article 3*

1. The producer shall be liable to pay compensation for death or personal injuries caused by a defect in his product.

2. Any person who has imported a product for putting it into circulation in the course of a business and any person who has presented a product as his product by causing his name, trademark or other distinguishing feature to appear on the product, shall be deemed to be producers for the purpose of this Convention and shall be liable as such.

3. When the product does not indicate the identity of any of the persons liable under paragraphs 1 and 2 of this Article, each supplier shall be deemed to be a producer for the purpose of this Convention and liable as such, unless he discloses, within a reasonable time, at the request of the claimant, the identity of the producer or of the person who supplied him with the product. The same shall apply, in the case of an imported product, if this product does not indicate the identity of the importer referred to in paragraph 2, even if the name of the producer is indicated.

4.    In    the    case    of  damage caused by a defect in a
product   incorporated   into another product, the producer   of   the   incorporated product and the producer
incorporating that product shall be liable.

5.    Where several persons are liable under this Convention   for the same damage, each shall be liable in
full (in solidum).

*Article 4*

1.    If   the injured person or the person entitled to
claim  compensation has by his own fault, contributed
to   the   damage,   the   compensation may be reduced or
disallowed having regard to all the circumstances.

2.    The    same    shall apply if a person, for whom the
injured   person   or the person entitled to claim compensation is responsible under national law, has contributed to the damage by his fault.

*Article 5*

1.    A   producer   shall not be liable under this Convention if he proves:

(a)    that   the product has not been put into circula-
       tion by him; or

(b)    that,   having regard to the circumstances, it is
       probable that the defect which caused the damage
       did   not   exist at the time when the product was
       put   into circulation by him or that this defect
       came into being afterwards; or

(c)    that   the   product   was neither manufactured for
       sale,   hire or any other form of distribution for
       the   economic   purposes   of   the   producer   nor
       manufactured or distributed in the course of his
       business.

2.    The liability of a producer shall not be reduced
when   the   damage   is   caused both by a defect in the
product and by the act or omission of a third party.

*Article 6*

Proceedings   for the recovery of the damages shall be
subject   to   a   limitation period of three years from
the   day   the claimant became aware or should reasonably   have   been   aware of the damage, the defect and
the identity of the producer.

*Article 7*

The right to compensation under this Convention
against a producer shall be extinguished if an action
is not brought within 10 years from the date on which
the producer put into circulation the individual
product which caused the damage.

*Article 8*

The liability of the producer under this Convention
cannot be excluded or limited by any exemption or
exoneration clause.

*Article 9*

This Convention shall not apply to:

(a)   the liability of producers *inter se* and their
      rights of recourse against third parties;

(b)   nuclear damage.

*Article 10*

Contracting States shall not adopt rules derogating
from this Convention, even if these rules are more
favourable to the victim.

*Article 11*

States may replace the liability of the producer, in
a principal or subsidiary way, wholly or in part, in
a general way, or for certain risks only, by the
liability of a guarantee fund or other form of
collective guarantee, provided that the victim shall
receive protection at least equivalent to the protection he would have had under the liability scheme
provided for by this Convention.

*Article 12*

This Convention shall not affect any rights which a
person suffering damage may have according to the
ordinary rules of the law of contractual and extra-
contractual liability including any rules concerning
the duties of a seller who sells goods in the course
of his business.

*Article 13*

1.   This Convention shall be open to signature by
the member States of the Council of Europe. It shall
be subject to ratification or acceptance. Instru-

ments of ratification or acceptance shall be deposited with the Secretary General of the Council of Europe.

2. This Convention shall enter into force on the first day of the month following the expiration of six months after the date of deposit of the third instrument of ratification or acceptance.

3. In respect of a signatory State ratifying or accepting subsequently, the Convention shall come into force on the first day of the month following the expiration of six months after the date of the deposit of its instrument of ratification or acceptance.

### Article 14

1. After the entry into force of this Convention, the Committee of Ministers of the Council of Europe may invite non-member States to accede.

2. Such accession shall be affected by depositing with the Secretary General of the Council of Europe an instrument of accession which shall take effect on the first day of the month following the expiration of six months after the date of its deposit.

### Article 15

1. Any Contracting State may, at the time of signature or when depositing its instrument of ratification, acceptance or accession, specify the territory to which this Convention shall apply.

2. Any Contracting State may, when depositing its instrument of ratification, acceptance or accession or at any later date, by declaration addressed to the Secretary General of the Council of Europe, extend this Convention to any other territory or territories specified in the declaration and for whose international relations it is responsible or on whose behalf it is authorised to give undertakings.

3. Any declaration made in pursuance of the preceding paragraph may, in respect of any territory mentioned in such declaration, be withdrawn according to the procedure laid down in Article 18 of this Convention.

### Article 16

1. Any Contracting State may, at the time of signature or when depositing its instrument of ratifica-

tion, acceptance or accession, or at any later date, by notification addressed to the Secretary General of the Council of Europe, declare that, in pursuance of an international agreement to which it is a Party, it will not consider imports from one or more specified States also Parties to that Agreement as imports for the purpose of paragraphs 2 and 3 of Article 3; in this case the person importing the product into any of these States from another State shall be deemed to be an importer for all the States Parties to this Agreement.

2.    Such a declaration may be withdrawn at any time in accordance with the procedure laid down in Article 18.

### Article 17

1.    No reservation shall be made to the provisions of this Convention except those mentioned in the Annex to this Convention.

2.    The Contracting State which has made one of the reservations mentioned in the Annex to this Convention may withdraw it by means of a declaration addressed to the Secretary General of the Council of Europe which shall become effective the first day of the month following the date of its receipt.

### Article 18

1.    Any Contracting State may, insofar as it is concerned, denounce this Convention by means of a notification addressed to the Secretary General of the Council of Europe.

2.    Such denunciation shall take effect on the first day of the month following the expiration of six months after the date of receipt by the Secretary General of such notification.

### Article 19

The Secretary General of the Council of Europe shall notify the member States of the Council and any State which has acceded to this Convention of:

(a)  any signature;

(b)  any deposit of an instrument of ratification, acceptance or accession;

(c)  any date of entry into force of this Convention in accordance with Article 13 therefore;

(d)  any reservations made in pursuance of the pro-
     visions of Article 17, paragraph 1;

(e)  withdrawal of any reservations carried out in
     pursuance of the provisions of Article 17,
     paragraph 2;

(f)  any communication received in pursuance of the
     provisions of Article 1, paragraph 2, Article
     15, paragraphs 2 and 3 and Article 16, para-
     graphs 1 and 2.

(g)  any notification received in pursuance of the
     provisions of Article 18 and the date on which
     denunciation takes effect.

In witness whereof, the undersigned being duly
authorised thereto, have signed this Convention.

Done at Strasbourg this 27th day of January 1977
in English and French, both texts being equally
authoritative, in a single copy, which shall remain
deposited in the archives of the Council of Europe.
The Secretary General shall transmit certified
copies of each of the signatory and acceding States.


**FOOTNOTE**

1    The Convention was adopted by the Committee of
     Ministers of the Council of Europe, Strasbourg,
     at the session of 20-29 September 1976, and was
     opened for signature on 27 January 1977.

**APPENDIX C**

<u>DRAFT BILL PROPOSED BY</u>
<u>ONTARIO LAW REFORM COMMISSION</u>

AN ACT TO IMPOSE LIABILITY
ON BUSINESS SUPPLIERS
OF DEFECTIVE PRODUCTS

HER MAJESTY, by and with the advice and consent of the Legislative Assembly of the Province of Ontario, enacts as follows:

*Interpretation*

1.(1)   In this Act,

(a)     "defective product" means a product that falls short of the standard that may reasonably be expected of it in all the circumstances.

(b)     "false statement" includes any mis-statement of fact, whether made by words, pictures, conduct or otherwise;

(c)     "product" means any tangible goods whether or not they are attached to or incorporated into real or personal property;

(d)     "to supply" means to make available or accessible by sale, gift, bailment or in any other way, and "supplied", "supplies" and "supplier" have corresponding meanings, but a person who transports a product is not by that act alone a supplier.

*Standards established by law*

(2) In determining whether or not a product is a defective product, any relevant standard established by law may be taken into account.

*Crown bound*

2.          The Crown is bound by this Act.

*Strict liability for defective products*

3.(1)   Where in  the course of his business a  person
supplies a product of a kind that it is his  business
to supply and the product is a defective product which
causes  personal injury or damage to  property,  that
person is liable in damages,

(a)       for the injury or damage so caused; and

(b)       for any economic loss directly consequent upon
          such injury or damage.

*Exception for business losses*

(2) A supplier  is not liable under clause (a) or  (b)
of  subsection 1 for damage to property used  in  the
course of carrying on a business.

*Strict liability for false statements
about products*

4.(1)   Where in  the course of his business a  person
supplies a product of a kind that it is his  business
to supply and makes a false statement concerning  the
product,  reliance upon which causes personal  injury
or  damage  to property, that person  is  liable   in
damages,

(a)       for the injury or damage so caused; and

(b)       for any economic loss directly consequent upon
          such injury or damage,

whether  or  not the reliance is that of  the  person
suffering the injury or damage.

*Exception for business losses*

(2) A supplier  is not liable under clause (a) or  (b)
of  subsection 1 for damage to property used  in  the
course of carrying on a business.

*New business and promotions*

5.       A person  may be liable under section 3  or  4
notwithstanding  that he has not previously  supplied
products of the same kind as the product supplied  or
that  he  supplied  the  product  for  promotional
purposes.

### *Contributory negligence*

6.(1) Where injury or damage is caused or contributed to partly by a supplier of a product under
section 3 or by reliance upon a false statement made
by a supplier concerning a product under section 4
and partly by the fault or neglect of the person
suffering the injury or damage, damages shall be
apportioned in accordance with the degree of the
responsibility of each for the injury or damage.

### *Where parties deemed equally responsible*

(2) Where under subsection 1 it is not practicable to determine the respective degree of responsibility of the supplier and of the person suffering
the injury or damage, the parties shall be deemed to
be equally responsible for the injury or damage
suffered, and damages shall be apportioned accordingly.

### *Joint tort feasors*

7.(1) Where injury or damage is caused or contributed to partly by a supplier of a product under
section 3 or by reliance upon a false statement made
by a supplier concerning a product under section 4
and partly by the fault or neglect of another
person, whether or not a supplier of the product,
for which that other person would be liable to the
person suffering the injury or damage, both the supplier and the other person are jointly and severally
liable to the person suffering the injury or damage,
but as between the supplier and the other person,
subject to any agreement express or implied, each
shall contribute to the amount of the damages in
accordance with the degree of the responsibility of
each for the injury or damage.

### *Where parties deemed equally responsible*

(2) Where under subsection 1 it is not practicable to determine the respective degree of responsibility of the supplier and of the other person, the
supplier and the other person shall be deemed to be
equally responsible for the injury or damage
suffered, and each shall contribute to the amount of
damages accordingly.

### Settlement

(3) A person who settles for a reasonable sum a claim for injury or damage under section 3 or 4 is entitled to claim contribution under subsection 1 and, in the event that the amount of the settlement is determined to be excessive, contribution shall be calculated in accordance with the amount for which the claim should have been settled.

### Indemnity by prior suppliers

8.    Subject to section 7 and to any agreement express or implied, a person who is liable or who settles for a reasonable sum a claim under this Act or otherwise for injury or damage caused by a product or by reliance upon a false statement made by a supplier concerning a product is entitled to be indemnified by any prior supplier of the product who would be liable under this Act for the injury or damage that gave rise to the liability and, in the event that the amount of the settlement is determined to be excessive, the indemnity shall be calculated in accordance with the amount for which the claim should have been settled.

### Limitation for contribution and indemnity

9.    Proceedings for contribution under section 7 or for indemnity under section 8 shall not be brought after,

(a)    the expiration of any limitation period that would bar an action against the person from whom contribution or indemnity is claimed; or

(b)    one year after judgment or settlement,

whichever is later.

### Restriction on liability void

10.    Any oral or written agreement, notice, statement or provision of any kind purporting to exclude or restrict liability under section 3 or 4 or to limit any remedy thereunder is void.

### Other rights not affected

11.    The rights and liabilities created by this Act are in addition to rights and liabilities otherwise provided by law.

## Trial by judge

12.     Any action under section 3 or 4 shall be tried by a judge without a jury.

## Extended jurisdiction

13.     An action may be brought under this Act where apart from this section the court would have jurisdiction or where the supplier at the time of the supply of the product carried on business in Ontario, and any party to such an action may be served out of Ontario in the manner prescribed by the rules of court.

## Choice of law

14.     In an action under this Act, the rights and liabilities of a supplier are governed by the internal law of Ontario where the internal law of Ontario would apart from this section apply or where the supplier at the time of the supply of the product carried on business in Ontario.

## Carrying on business

15.     A supplier of defective product or a supplier of a product who makes a false statement concerning that product shall be deemed to have carried on business in Ontario for the purposes of sections 13 and 14.

(a)     where the product or identical products supplied by him were available or accessible in Ontario through commercial channels with his consent express or implied; or

(b)     where the supplier has acted in any way to further the supply of the product or identical products in Ontario.

## Rights of dependants

16.     Where a person is injured or killed under circumstances where the person is entitled under section 3 or 4 to recover damages, or would have been so entitled if not killed, the spouse as defined in Part II of The Family Law Reform Act, 1978, children, grandchildren, parents, grandparents, brothers and sisters of the person are entitled to recover their pecuniary loss resulting from the injury or death from the person from whom the person injured or killed is entitled to recover or would have been entitled if not killed, and to

maintain an action for the purpose in a court of competent jurisdiction, and Part V, except sub-section 1 of section 60, of *The Family Law Reform Act, 1978* applies *mutatis mutandis* to any such action.

### Application of Act

17.    This Act applies only to injury or damage occurring on or after the day on which this Act comes into force.

### Short title

18.    The short title of this Act is *The Products Liability Act, 198* .